Artificial Intelligence

A Journey into the world of Intelligence Machines

About the Book

Welcome to the enthralling world of "AI Explorers: Embarking on a Journey into the World of Artificial Intelligence." This book is designed especially for young readers to unlock the mysteries of Artificial Intelligence (AI) and embark on a thrilling adventure like never before.

In this captivating exploration, readers will delve into the very heart of AI, discovering how machines are becoming smarter and more capable of performing tasks that once seemed impossible. From understanding the basics of AI to delving into the wonders of Machine Learning, Natural Language Processing, Robotics, Computer Vision, and the ethical considerations surrounding AI, this book offers a comprehensive and enjoyable journey through cutting-edge technology.

Through engaging language and relatable examples, young learners will grasp the concept of how AI allows machines to learn, think, and interact like humans. They'll dive into the world of Machine Learning, uncovering the secrets of how AI models can predict the future and uncover hidden patterns in data.

Finally, the book raises important questions about the ethical implications of AI. Young readers will be encouraged to think critically about the responsible use of AI, considering matters like bias, privacy, and fairness in AI applications.

Through captivating stories, interactive activities, and thought-provoking discussions, "AI Explorers" seeks to inspire young minds to embrace AI's wonders responsibly. So, buckle up and get ready for an exhilarating journey into the world of Artificial Intelligence, where imagination and innovation know no bounds!

By Abdulillah Faruqi

TABLE OF CONTENT

                             Page

1. Introduction to Artificial Intelligence……3
2. Machine Learning Basics …………………23
3. Natural Language Processing (NLP)……..44
4. Introduction to Computer Vision …………74
5. Introduction to Robotics…………………..89
6. Ethics and Artificial Intelligence…………104
7. Glossory ……………………………………117

Module 1: Introduction to Artificial Intelligence

What is Artificial Intelligence?

Artificial Intelligence (AI) is a branch of computer science focused on creating machines that can perform tasks that typically require human intelligence. It involves designing algorithms and models that enable computers to learn from data, reason, and make decisions, mimicking human cognitive abilities."

Artificial Intelligence (AI) refers to the development and implementation of intelligent systems that possess the ability to perform tasks requiring human-like cognitive abilities. It involves the creation of computer programs and algorithms that enable machines to perceive, reason, learn, and make decisions or take actions based on data and experiences. AI aims to replicate and augment human intelligence, enabling machines to understand, adapt, and interact with their environment in a way that is typically associated with human intelligence.

At its core, AI seeks to build intelligent systems capable of exhibiting characteristics such as:

- **Problem-solving**
- **Pattern recognition**
- **Natural language processing**
- **Knowledge representation, and machine learning.**

AI encompasses a broad range of subfields and approaches including:

Machine learning **Natural language processing**
Computer vision   **Robotics**   **Expert systems**

It finds applications in numerous domains, such as healthcare, finance, transportation, education, entertainment, and more.

The goal of AI is to create machines that can autonomously learn, reason, and adapt, leading to advanced problem-solving capabilities and enhanced decision-making. While AI continues to advance rapidly, it is important to ensure ethical development and use of AI technologies, addressing concerns around privacy, bias, transparency, and the impact of AI on society.

Module 1: Introduction to Artificial Intelligence

Simplified Understanding of AI

Computer Science

| Machine Learning | Natural Language Processing | Computer Vision | Robotics |

Speech Recognition/ Pattern

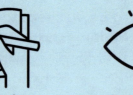
Read and Write

See from Eyes

Moving Around

Module 1: Introduction to Artificial Intelligence

Examples of AI

Text Editors or Autocorrect

Maps and Navigation

Facial Detection and Recognition

Search and Recommendation

Social Media

Weather Forecast

In summary, AI is a multidisciplinary field focused on developing intelligent systems that can mimic human intelligence, process information, and perform tasks autonomously. It holds immense potential to revolutionize various aspects of our lives and contribute to significant advancements in technology and society.

Intelligence

Intelligence is the ability to learn, reason, and solve problems effectively. It involves understanding and adapting to new situations, using knowledge and experiences to make informed decisions. Intelligent individuals can analyze information, think critically, and apply creativity to find innovative solutions. Intelligence comes in various forms, such as logical-mathematical, linguistic, spatial, and interpersonal. It's not just about memorizing facts but also about using acquired knowledge to navigate the world and interact with others. Emphasizing continuous learning and curiosity, intelligence is a valuable trait that helps individuals grow, excel in academics, and succeed in various aspects of life.

Artificial Intelligence

Artificial Intelligence (AI) is a fascinating field of computer science that aims to make machines smart like humans. It involves creating computer programs and algorithms that can learn from data, reason, and make decisions. AI enables computers to understand language, recognize images, play games, and even drive cars autonomously. It is used in virtual assistants like Siri and chatbots on websites. AI helps us in daily life by providing personalized recommendations, predicting weather, and detecting spam emails. As technology advances, AI is becoming more essential in shaping our future, revolutionizing industries, and making our lives easier and more exciting.

To sum up, intelligence is a vital part of how our minds work, involving various abilities that help us learn and navigate the world. On the other hand, AI aims to make machines act like humans, doing things that need intelligence. Although AI has come a long way, achieving full human-like intelligence is still difficult. It's essential to be mindful of ethics while developing AI, so we can use it to make the world a better place.

Module 1: Introduction to Artificial Intelligence

Intelligence, Knowledge, and the Continuum of Learning

- **The Relationship Between Intelligence and Knowledge:**

Intelligence is the innate ability of the mind to acquire, understand, and use knowledge. While intelligence is the capacity, knowledge is the accumulation of facts, information, and skills that we gain through experience or education. One might consider intelligence as the vessel, while knowledge fills it up.

- **Knowledge and Continuous Learning:**

Knowledge is not a static entity. The world changes, innovations emerge, and fresh insights appear daily. As such, the most fruitful minds are those that engage in continuous learning. Continuous learning is the act of persistently expanding one's knowledge base, adapting to new circumstances, and preparing oneself for uncharted challenges. In a world dominated by rapid technological advancements, continuous learning is not just a luxury; it's a necessity.

- **The Importance of Learning for Humankind:**

Throughout history, it's been evident that societies that prioritize learning progress faster and more sustainably. From decoding the mysteries of DNA to landing on Mars, every achievement is a testament to humankind's insatiable thirst for knowledge. Learning doesn't just propel technological advancements; it fosters empathy, cultivates cultures, and bridges divides. The pursuit of knowledge has, and always will be, our guiding light towards a brighter future.

Module 1: Introduction to Artificial Intelligence

Types of Artificial Intelligence

Narrow

Strong

Super AI

- **Narrow or Weak Artificial Intelligence**

Narrow AI, often referred to as Weak AI, represents AI systems designed and trained for a specific task or a narrow range of tasks. These systems are highly specialized and excel in performing well-defined tasks, such as image recognition, language translation, or playing board games like chess or Go. However, they lack the ability to generalize their knowledge or skills to tasks outside their predefined scope. It is like a robot that's excellent at one thing, like solving math problems or recognizing pictures of animals. It's really good at that particular task, but it doesn't know much about anything else. Think of it as a super-skilled expert in a single subject, like a math genius or a chess champion. It can do amazing things in its specialty, but it's not good at everything else.

Narrow AI systems operate under a limited set of constraints and do not possess consciousness, self-awareness, or the ability to understand context beyond their specialized domain. They rely on data and algorithms to make decisions or provide responses, and their performance is typically evaluated based on their accuracy and efficiency within their designated tasks.

Despite their limitations, Narrow AI systems have proven to be incredibly useful and have paved the way for more advanced AI systems in the future. As AI continues to evolve, researchers and developers are working towards creating more sophisticated AI systems that can perform a wider range of tasks and possess greater levels of intelligence and autonomy.

Module 1: Introduction to Artificial Intelligence

Types of Artificial Intelligence

- **General or Strong Artificial Intelligence**

General AI, also known as Strong AI or AGI (Artificial General Intelligence), represents a form of AI that possesses human-like cognitive abilities. A true General AI system would have the capacity to understand, learn, and apply knowledge across a wide range of tasks, much like a human being. It would exhibit general intelligence, adaptability, and the ability to reason and learn from experiences, enabling it to excel in diverse domains.

Strong AI, is like a robot with general smarts. Picture a robot that can do all sorts of things, just like a human. It can learn new things, solve different problems, and even understand jokes and stories. It's like having a robot friend who's really clever and can help with many tasks, from homework to making decisions.

The development of General AI would be a major breakthrough in the field of AI and could have a significant impact on society. It has the potential to revolutionize industries such as healthcare, transportation, and education. However, General AI also comes with its own set of challenges and ethical concerns, such as the risk of it becoming uncontrollable or developing its own goals that conflict with human interests.

Types of Artificial Intelligence

- **Superintelligence**

Superintelligence refers to a hypothetical AI system that surpasses human intelligence in all aspects. It represents a level of AI development where machines possess not only general intelligence but do so to an extent far beyond human capabilities. Super intelligent AI would have the ability to perform tasks, make decisions, and solve problems at a level that is currently inconceivable for humans.

Superintelligence is like a robot that's super, super smart - even smarter than the smartest human beings. This robot can do everything incredibly well, from solving complex problems to inventing new things. It's like a superhero of AI, and it can outthink and outperform humans in nearly everything.

The concept of superintelligence raises complex ethical and existential questions, as such a system could potentially outperform humans in almost every intellectual endeavor, leading to concerns about control, safety, and the implications for society. It's important to note that while Narrow AI is prevalent in our daily lives, General AI and Superintelligence remain aspirational goals in the field of artificial intelligence, with significant research and development required to achieve them.

Keep in mind that right now, we mostly have Narrow AI in our daily lives, like the voice assistants on our phones. Scientists and engineers are working hard to make General AI and, maybe one day, Superintelligence a reality. But for now, we're mostly surrounded by super-smart specialists, and that's pretty amazing too!

Despite the challenges and uncertainties surrounding the development of superintelligence, many researchers and organizations are working towards achieving this goal. Some of the key areas of focus for AI development include improving machine learning algorithms, developing more advanced hardware and processing power, and exploring new approaches to AI development.

Artificial Intelligence impact in our daily life

- **AI in Health Care:**

AI is making significant strides in healthcare, improving diagnosis, treatment, and patient care. Machine learning algorithms analyze medical images, assisting in early detection of diseases like cancer. AI-powered chatbots and virtual nurses provide personalized medical advice and support. Predictive analytics aid in identifying at-risk patients and optimizing healthcare resource allocation. However, ethical considerations, privacy concerns, and ensuring AI's reliability remain critical challenges.

- **AI in Transportation:**

Autonomous vehicles, driven by AI, promise safer and more efficient transportation systems. Self-driving cars are being tested to reduce accidents caused by human error. AI-powered traffic management optimizes traffic flow, reducing congestion. Delivery drones enhance last-mile logistics. The impact of AI on employment in transportation and potential regulatory hurdles require careful attention.

- **AI in Education:**

AI technologies are transforming the education landscape, personalizing learning experiences, and supporting educators. Intelligent tutoring systems offer tailored learning paths and feedback to students. AI-enabled chatbots assist with administrative tasks and address student inquiries. Data analytics provide insights to improve educational outcomes. Balancing AI's role with human interaction in education and addressing accessibility concerns are vital considerations.

Module 1: Introduction to Artificial Intelligence

Notable figures in AI research

The field of Artificial Intelligence (AI) owes its progress and advancements to the significant contributions of notable figures in AI research. These visionaries and pioneers have shaped the direction of AI, introducing groundbreaking ideas and developing key technologies. Here are some of the most influential figures in AI research and their contributions:

Alan Turing (1912-1954):

Alan Turing is considered the father of computer science and artificial intelligence. His work on the Turing machine laid the foundation for computation theory, providing the conceptual basis for modern computers and AI. Turing's famous "Turing Test" proposed a criterion for determining a machine's ability to exhibit human-like intelligence.

John McCarthy (1927-2011):

Known as the "father of AI," John McCarthy organized the Dartmouth Workshop in 1956, which is considered the birth of AI as a field of study. He coined the term "artificial intelligence" and made significant contributions to symbolic reasoning and the development of the Lisp programming language.

Marvin Minsky (1927-2016):

Marvin Minsky was a cognitive scientist and co-founder of the MIT AI Laboratory. He worked on early AI systems, including the first neural network simulator and the "tentacle arm" robotic hand. His research on artificial neural networks laid the groundwork for future developments in deep learning.

Key milestones in the development of AI

Key milestones in the development of AI mark significant breakthroughs and advancements that have shaped the evolution of artificial intelligence. These milestones represent critical moments where researchers and innovators made groundbreaking discoveries, laying the foundation for the field's growth. Below are some key milestones in AI's development:

Logic Theorist (1956):
Allen Newell and Herbert A. Simon developed Logic Theorist, the first AI program capable of proving mathematical theorems. This demonstrated that machines could manipulate symbols and reason effectively.

General Problem Solver (GPS) (1959):
Newell and Simon also developed GPS, a program capable of solving a wide range of problems using means-ends analysis and heuristic techniques, showcasing the potential of AI for problem-solving.

ELIZA (1966):
Joseph Weizenbaum created ELIZA, a natural language processing program simulating a psychotherapist. ELIZA engaged users in human-like conversations, marking an early example of chatbot technology.

Shakey the Robot (1970s):
Developed at Stanford Research Institute, Shakey was one of the first robots to perceive its environment, plan actions, and navigate autonomously, making it a pioneering example of AI in robotics.

Expert Systems (1970s-1980s):
The development of expert systems, like MYCIN for medical diagnosis and DENDRAL for chemical analysis, demonstrated AI's potential in emulating human expertise and decision-making in specialized domains.

Backpropagation Algorithm (1986):
The backpropagation algorithm, developed by Geoffrey Hinton and others, enabled training artificial neural networks effectively, leading to the resurgence of interest in neural networks and deep learning.

IBM's Deep Blue (1997):
IBM's Deep Blue defeated world chess champion Garry Kasparov, showcasing the power of AI in defeating human experts in complex strategic games.

Watson's Jeopardy! Victory (2011):
IBM's Watson AI system won the TV quiz show Jeopardy!, demonstrating the ability of AI to understand natural language and process vast amounts of information.

AlphaGo (2016):
DeepMind's AlphaGo defeated world champion Go player Lee Sedol, indicating AI's remarkable capabilities in mastering complex games with a high level of strategic thinking and intuition.

AI Applications in various domains

Artificial Intelligence (AI) has rapidly become an integral part of our daily lives, impacting various aspects and enhancing the way we interact with technology and the world around us. From personal assistants to recommendation systems, AI applications have proliferated, revolutionizing industries and improving user experiences. Here are some prominent examples of AI applications in everyday life:

Virtual Assistants:
AI-powered virtual assistants like Apple's Siri, Amazon's Alexa, and Google Assistant have become ubiquitous on smartphones and smart speakers. These intelligent agents can perform tasks based on voice commands, such as setting reminders, providing weather updates, answering questions, and controlling smart home devices.

Personalized Recommendations:
AI recommendation systems are prevalent in online platforms like Netflix, Amazon, and YouTube. By analyzing user behavior and preferences, these systems suggest personalized content, such as movies, products, or videos, enhancing user engagement and satisfaction.

Natural Language Processing (NLP):
NLP allows machines to understand and interact with human language. AI applications with NLP capabilities enable voice recognition, sentiment analysis, and language translation, powering features like speech-to-text and chatbots in customer service.

Social Media and Content Curation:
AI algorithms play a vital role in social media platforms by curating content, showing relevant posts, and filtering out spam. AI helps identify abusive content and potentially harmful information, contributing to a safer online environment.

Navigation and Transportation:
AI-powered navigation applications, such as Google Maps and Waze, optimize routes and provide real-time traffic updates. In the transportation sector, AI is being integrated into autonomous vehicles to improve safety and efficiency on the roads.

Healthcare and Medical Diagnostics:
AI applications in healthcare assist with medical diagnostics and decision-making. AI algorithms analyze medical images, such as X-rays and MRIs, to aid in early disease detection. AI-driven virtual health assistants provide personalized health advice and information.

Fraud Detection and Cybersecurity:
AI technologies are crucial in combating fraud and enhancing cybersecurity. AI algorithms analyze vast amounts of data to detect suspicious activities in financial transactions, helping prevent fraudulent transactions and protect sensitive information.

Smart Home Devices:
AI is at the core of smart home devices and Internet of Things (IoT) technologies. From smart thermostats that adjust temperature preferences to AI-powered security cameras that recognize and differentiate between people and pets, these devices enhance home automation and security.

Entertainment and Gaming:
AI has a significant impact on the entertainment industry. AI-driven content recommendation systems suggest music, movies, and shows tailored to individual tastes. In gaming, AI-powered characters and opponents provide challenging and engaging experiences.

The applications of AI in everyday life continue to expand, driven by ongoing research and technological advancements. While these AI technologies offer tremendous benefits, it is essential to address ethical considerations and privacy concerns to ensure responsible and beneficial use of AI in our daily interactions and experiences.

Module 1: Introduction to Artificial Intelligence

Programming Language of AI

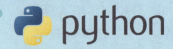 

1. Python:
Python is arguably the most popular programming language in the field of artificial intelligence. It is known for its simplicity and readability, making it an excellent choice for both beginners and experienced developers. Python has a vast ecosystem of libraries and frameworks specifically designed for AI and machine learning, such as TensorFlow, PyTorch, and scikit-learn. These libraries provide pre-built tools and functions for tasks like neural network development, data analysis, and natural language processing. Python's versatility, extensive community support, and rich set of AI libraries make it the go-to language for many AI projects.

2. R:
R is another programming language commonly used in AI, particularly for statistical analysis and data visualization. It excels in handling and analyzing data, which is a crucial aspect of AI and machine learning. Data scientists often use R for tasks like data cleansing, exploration, and statistical modeling. R's strength lies in its data manipulation and visualization packages, such as ggplot2 and dplyr, making it a valuable tool in AI research involving data analysis and statistical modeling.

3. Java:
Java is a versatile, platform-independent language that finds applications in various domains, including AI. While it may not be as popular as Python in the AI community, Java is still used in AI projects, especially in areas where performance and scalability are critical. Java is known for its robustness and ability to handle large-scale AI applications. It's commonly used in enterprise-level AI solutions, including chatbots, recommendation systems, and data processing pipelines. Additionally, Java offers libraries like Deeplearning4j for deep learning tasks.

These programming languages, Python, R, and Java, each have their unique strengths and are chosen based on the specific requirements of an AI project. Python, with its extensive libraries and ease of use, is particularly dominant in the machine learning and deep learning domains. R is favored for data-centric AI tasks, while Java is chosen for projects that require scalability and performance.

Module 1: Introduction of Artificial Intelligence

1. **What is Artificial Intelligence (AI)?** ✓ Check on the right answer

	a) The study of natural languages
	b) A branch of computer science that can perform human-like intelligence
	c) The study of biological organisms and ecosystems

2. **Which of the following is NOT an example of AI application in everyday life?**

	a) Google Map
	b) Search and Recommendation
	c) Traditional calculators

3. **Which is not a subfield of Artificial Intelligence**

	a) Machine learning
	b) Natural Language Processing
	c) Building Web Application

Module 1:
Introduction of Artificial Intelligence

4. Which AI application involves computers understanding and interpreting human language? ✓ Check on the right answer

	a) Image recognition
	b) Speech synthesis
	c) Natural Language Processing (NLP)

5. Which one of these is not an area of AI?

	a) Web Designing
	b) Pattern recognition
	c) Knowledge representation, and machine learning.

6. Who is the father of AI

	a) John McCarthy
	b) Jon McCarthy
	c) Gram Bell

Page: 21

Module 1:
Introduction of Artificial Intelligence

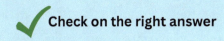 Check on the right answer

7. What makes Artificial Intelligence such a transformative technology?

	a) It can replace human creativity and problem-solving abilities
	b) It enables machines to learn, adapt, and make intelligent decisions from data
	c) It makes computers more expensive and difficult to maintain

8. What is technology name of ChatBots

	a) Eliza
	b) Logic Theorist
	c) Shakey the Robot

9. What is are of MYCN Expert System for ?

	a) Medical Science
	b) Industrial and Innovation
	c) Farming and Agricultural

Module 2:
Machine Learning Basics

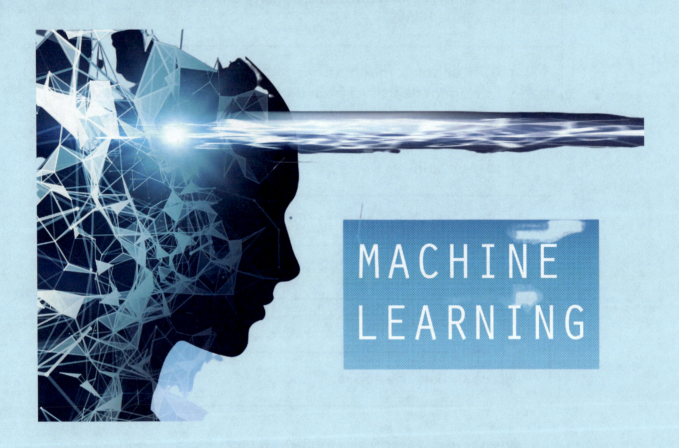

Module 2: Machine Learning Basics

What is Machine Learning?

"Machine learning is like teaching computers to learn and make choices on their own. It uses data and patterns to improve and get smarter over time, just like how you learn from your experiences. It's what makes things like voice assistants and self-driving cars possible!"

Machine learning is an application of Artificial Intelligence where we give machines access to data and let them use that data to learn for themselves. It's basically getting a computer to perform a task without explicitly being programmed to do so.

At its core, Machine Learning operates on the principle of pattern recognition. It enables computers to identify meaningful patterns and relationships within vast amounts of data, which can be used to make accurate predictions or categorize new and unseen data. Unlike traditional programming, where specific instructions are provided to solve a problem, Machine Learning models learn to generalize from examples, allowing them to handle diverse scenarios.

The role of Machine Learning in everyday technology is pervasive and diverse. One common application is in recommendation systems. Whenever we receive personalized product recommendations on online shopping platforms, watch suggestions on streaming services, or friend recommendations on social media, we are experiencing Machine Learning in action. These systems analyze our past preferences and behaviors to suggest items or content that align with our interests, enhancing our overall user experience.

Module 2: Machine Learning Basics

Moreover, Machine Learning is at the heart of virtual assistants like Siri, Alexa, and Google Assistant. These intelligent agents process natural language and respond to our queries, translating our speech into actionable commands. As they interact with us, these virtual assistants learn from our interactions and improve their responses over time, adapting to our preferences and needs.

Machine Learning also plays a vital role in image and speech recognition. Smartphones, cameras, and other devices use ML algorithms to identify objects in images, enabling features like face recognition or scene detection. Additionally, speech recognition technologies convert our spoken words into text, powering voice search and dictation functionalities.

Machine learning gives computers and machines access to data (information), so they can then learn for themselves without a human having to program, type in or speak a command. Machine learning described in simple words, can happen in 3 ways:

- **Computers watch and observe what others do, then copy that action.**
- **Computers watch and observe and then use logic to make their own decision based on previous experiences with "data".**
- **Computers learn from their previous mistakes.**

In summary, Machine Learning is a transformative technology that empowers computers to learn, adapt, and make intelligent decisions based on data. Its applications touch many aspects of our lives, making our interactions with technology more personalized, efficient, and intuitive. As Machine Learning continues to advance, its influence on various industries and everyday technology will only grow, shaping a future where intelligent systems become even more integrated into our daily routines.

Module 2: Machine Learning Basics

Short Definition

Machine learning is a subset of AI which provides machines the ability to learn automatically & improve from experience without being explicitly programmed

Machine Learning Process

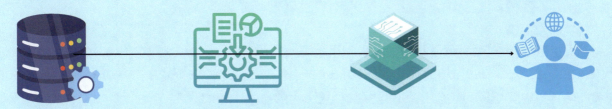

Database → Training the Machine → Building a Model → Predictive Outcome

Step 1: The Database
Imagine you have a huge collection of photos of animals—cats, dogs, and birds. This collection is like your database, filled with lots of information. In machine learning, we call this data. It's like the raw material we use to teach the computer.

Step 2: Training the Machine
Now, we want the computer to recognize these animals, just like you can. But the computer doesn't know anything yet. So, we show it the pictures and tell it what's in each picture. We say, "This is a cat," "This is a dog," and so on. We do this with thousands of pictures until the computer gets really good at recognizing them. This part is like teaching the computer.

Step 3: Building a Model
The computer learns from the pictures, and it starts to see patterns. For example, it notices that cats often have pointy ears, and dogs have floppy ears. It also learns about colors, sizes, and shapes. All this learning is put together into what we call a model. Think of it as a special brain made of math that helps the computer make sense of things.

Short Definition

Step 4: Achieving the Predicted Outcome

Now comes the exciting part! We give the computer a new picture, one it has never seen before. We ask it, "What's in this picture?" Using its model and all the things it learned, the computer makes a guess. It might say, "I think it's a cat!" And guess what? It's often right!

That's how machine learning works. It's like teaching a computer to see, learn, and make smart guesses. We use this for all sorts of things, like recognizing faces, predicting weather, or even suggesting movies you might like.

So, in simple terms, machine learning is like teaching a computer using pictures and data, and then it becomes really good at figuring things out on its own. It's a bit like magic, but it's all about patterns and learning!

Module 2: Machine Learning Basics

How Does It Work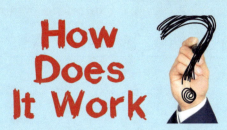

Imagine you have a friend named Alex, who loves to play games on their computer. Alex wants to teach the computer to recognize if a picture shows a cute dog or a grumpy cat. But instead of telling the computer how to do it, Alex decides to play a fun game with the computer.

- **Collecting Pictures:** First, Alex gathers lots of pictures of cute dogs and grumpy cats. These pictures will be used to teach the computer.

- **Labeling the Pictures:** Alex looks at each picture and writes a label on it, saying whether it's a cute dog or a grumpy cat. This helps the computer know what each picture represents.

- **Playing the Guessing Game:** Now, Alex shows the pictures to the computer one by one. The computer looks at the pictures and tries to guess if it's a cute dog or a grumpy cat based on the labels Alex provided.

- **Learning from Mistakes:** Sometimes, the computer makes mistakes and guesses wrong. But that's okay because Alex helps the computer learn from those mistakes. For example, if the computer thinks a grumpy cat is a cute dog, Alex kindly corrects it.

- **Getting Smarter:** The more pictures the computer sees and the more mistakes it learns from, the better it becomes at guessing. With time, it starts recognizing patterns like fluffy ears for dogs or pointy whiskers for cats.

- **Making New Friends:** Now, after playing this game with many pictures, the computer becomes really good at recognizing cute dogs and grumpy cats. It can look at new pictures and confidently say whether it's a dog or a cat.

This game Alex played with the computer is how machine learning works! The computer learned from the pictures and labels to get better at identifying dogs and cats. Machine learning can be used to solve all sorts of exciting problems, like helping doctors diagnose diseases or even suggesting new games for Alex to play!

Module 2: Machine Learning Basics

Real Time: Virtual Assistants

You might have heard of virtual assistants like Siri, Alexa, or Google Assistant. These helpful AI companions are excellent examples of how machine learning can be applied in our daily lives.

Listening and Learning: Virtual assistants use machine learning to understand and respond to your voice commands. When you talk to them, they listen and learn from what you say.

Natural Language Processing: They use a technology called "Natural Language Processing" to understand human language better. It helps them recognize words, phrases, and the meaning behind your questions or requests.

Training with Data: These virtual assistants have been trained on vast amounts of data containing various speech patterns, accents, and languages. This training helps them adapt to different users and understand a wide range of queries.

Improving with Use: As more people use virtual assistants, they keep learning and getting better at understanding our commands. They learn from interactions with millions of users around the world.

Personalization: Virtual assistants can personalize their responses based on your previous interactions. For example, they can remember your preferences, such as your favorite music, and use that knowledge to give you better recommendations.

Assisting in Daily Tasks: By using machine learning, virtual assistants can help with tasks like setting reminders, answering questions, playing music, and controlling smart home devices, making our lives more convenient and enjoyable.

Virtual assistants are just one example of how machine learning enhances our daily experiences by creating intelligent and personalized interactions with technology. They are always learning and evolving to be more helpful companions in our everyday lives.

Module 2: Machine Learning Basics
Machine Learning Techniques

Machine learning techniques are methods and algorithms used to enable computers to learn from data and make predictions or decisions without being explicitly programmed. There are various machine learning techniques, and they can be broadly categorized into three main types: supervised learning, unsupervised learning, and reinforcement learning. Here's an overview of these techniques:

1. Supervised Learning:

Common algorithms in supervised learning include:
- Linear Regression
- Logistic Regression
- Decision Trees
- Support Vector Machines (SVM)
- Neural Networks (Deep Learning)

2. Unsupervised Learning:

Common algorithms in unsupervised learning include:
- K-means Clustering
- Hierarchical Clustering
- Principal Component Analysis (PCA)
- Autoencoders (Deep Learning)

3. Reinforcement Learning:

Common algorithms in reinforcement learning include:
- Q-Learning
- Deep Q-Networks (DQN)
- Policy Gradient Methods

Besides these main types, there are also hybrid techniques and specialized algorithms used for specific tasks, such as natural language processing (NLP), computer vision, and recommendation systems. Machine learning techniques are continually evolving, and researchers are always exploring new methods to improve performance and address diverse real-world challenges.

Module 2: Machine Learning Basics

Supervised Learning

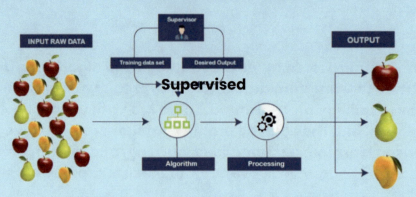

Supervised learning is a type of machine learning where a computer is taught to make predictions or decisions based on examples that have known outcomes. It's like having a teacher guiding the computer throughout the learning process.

Imagine you want to teach a computer to identify different fruits. You show the computer many pictures of fruits like apples, bananas, and oranges, and you tell it what each fruit is. This labeled data (the pictures with their corresponding names) serves as the teacher's guidance.

The computer uses this labeled data to learn patterns and features that distinguish each fruit. For example, it might learn that apples are round and have a stem, while bananas are long and curved.

Once the computer has learned from these examples, you can test it with new pictures of fruits it has never seen before. The computer will try to predict which fruit is in each new picture based on what it learned during training.

Supervised learning is widely used in various applications, like identifying spam emails, recognizing handwriting, diagnosing diseases from medical images, and even predicting the weather. It's a powerful method that allows computers to learn and make accurate decisions by following the guidance of labeled examples provided by humans.

Module 2: Machine Learning Basics

Supervised Learning

Common algorithms in supervised learning

Linear Regression:

Linear Regression is a statistical method that models the relationship between a dependent variable and one or more independent variables. It predicts continuous values based on the linear relationship between the variables.

Logistic Regression:

Unlike Linear Regression which predicts continuous values, Logistic Regression is used for binary classification tasks. It estimates the probability that a given instance belongs to a particular category.

Decision Trees:

Decision Trees split the data into subsets based on the most significant attributes, making decisions at every node. They are graphical representations that make decisions based on asking a series of questions.

Support Vector Machines (SVM):

SVM is a classification (and regression) algorithm that aims to find the optimal hyperplane which best divides a dataset into classes. It is especially powerful for classifying non-linear data. SVM is like drawing the best line or curve to separate two groups of things. It's a tool that helps computers classify and sort things based on the patterns they see

Neural Networks (Deep Learning):

Neural Networks are algorithms inspired by the structure of the human brain. They consist of layers of interconnected nodes (neurons). Deep Learning refers to Neural Networks with a large number of layers, allowing them to learn complex patterns from vast amounts of data.

Module 2: Machine Learning Basics

Un-Supervised Learning

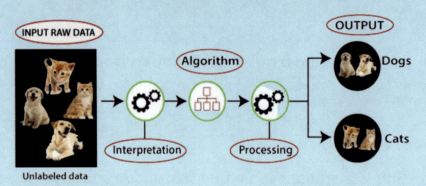

Unsupervised learning is another type of machine learning, but it's a bit different from supervised learning. In unsupervised learning, the computer learns from data without any specific guidance or labeled examples.

Imagine you have a big box of colorful toys, but you don't know how many different types of toys are there or which ones belong together. Your task is to sort these toys into groups based on their similarities, but you don't have any labels telling you what each toy is.

In unsupervised learning, the computer does something similar. It takes a bunch of data, like pictures or numbers, and tries to find patterns or similarities without anyone telling it what each data point represents. It groups similar things together and tries to make sense of the data on its own.

For example, if you gave the computer pictures of animals, it might group them into categories like "dogs," "cats," and "birds" based on the similarities it finds in the images.

Unsupervised learning is useful when we have lots of data, but we don't know what it all means. It helps us discover hidden patterns, group similar items, and gain insights from data without any explicit instructions.

Module 2: Machine Learning Basics

Un-Supervised Learning

Common algorithms in unsupervised learning

K-means Clustering

Imagine you have a box of crayons without labels. K-means is like trying to group these crayons by similar colors, even if you don't know the exact names of those colors.

Hierarchical Clustering

Think of this as organizing toys into boxes. First, you group toys that are very similar, like action figures. Then, you might group those boxes into bigger boxes, like "toys with characters."

Principal Component Analysis (PCA)

PCA is a statistical method used to simplify and reduce the dimensions of large datasets. It does this while retaining as much of the original data's variance (or information) as possible. Imagine organizing toys into boxes. Begin by grouping similar toys, such as action figures, and then place those boxes into larger boxes, such as "toys with characters."

Autoencoders (Deep Learning):

Think of a toy that you can take apart and then put back together. Autoencoders do something similar with information: they break it down and then try to rebuild it.

Module 2: Machine Learning Basics

Reinforcement Learning

Reinforcement learning is different from supervised and unsupervised learning. It involves an agent that interacts with an environment and learns by receiving feedback (rewards or punishments) for its actions. The goal is for the agent to learn the best actions to take to maximize the cumulative rewards over time.

Example: Training a Dog to Fetch the Ball

Imagine you want to train your dog, to fetch a ball and bring it back to you. You decide to use reinforcement learning to teach him this fun trick.

Agent: the Dog

Environment: Your backyard or a play area with a ball

Rewards: Positive reward (treat or praise) for successfully fetching the ball, negative reward (gentle "no" or ignoring) for not fetching the ball

Steps:

Initial State: Start by showing Max the ball and getting him excited about it. This is the initial state of the environment.

Action: Throw the ball a short distance and ask Max to fetch it.

Reward: If Max successfully fetches the ball and brings it back to you, give him a positive reward, such as a treat or lots of praise. This is the reward for his good action.

Feedback Loop: Repeat steps 2 and 3 multiple times. Each time Max fetches the ball, reward him positively. If he doesn't fetch the ball or gets distracted, give a gentle "no" or ignore him.

Learning: Dog will start to associate fetching the ball with positive rewards. He will want to repeat the action to receive more treats and praise.

Reinforcement: As Dog continues to fetch the ball and receive positive rewards, his behavior will strengthen through reinforcement learning. He learns that fetching the ball leads to good things.

Improvement: With consistent training and reinforcement, Max becomes more skilled at fetching the ball and bringing it back to you.

Generalization: Over time, Dog learns to fetch the ball even without treats, as he now associates the action itself with a positive experience.

Module 2: Machine Learning Basics

Reinforcement Learning

Common algorithms in Reinforcement learning

Q-Learning

Imagine playing a video game where you're trying to maximize your score. In Q-Learning, the game character learns which actions (like jumping or running) give the best rewards in different situations. Over time, it builds a guide (called the Q-table) that tells it which action is best to take in each situation to get the highest score

Deep Q-Networks (DQN)

Building on Q-Learning, DQN uses deep learning (neural networks) to handle more complex games or situations. Instead of a simple guide, it uses a neural network to predict the best actions. Think of it as giving our game character a more advanced brain to make decisions.

Policy Gradient Methods

Instead of just focusing on the best action in each situation, Policy Gradient Methods try to learn a strategy (or policy) for the whole game. It's like training a soccer player not just to shoot goals but to understand the entire game flow, adjusting their actions based on the situation.

Benefits of Machine Learning:

Automation: Machine learning allows computers to automate tasks that would be time-consuming or challenging for humans. This leads to increased efficiency and productivity in various industries.

Accurate Predictions: Machine learning models can analyze vast amounts of data and make predictions with high accuracy. This helps in making informed decisions and solving complex problems more effectively.

Personalization: Machine learning enables personalized experiences for users. It powers recommendation systems in streaming platforms, online shopping, and social media, tailoring content and suggestions to individual preferences.

Medical Advancements: In the healthcare field, machine learning helps in diagnosing diseases, identifying patterns in medical images, and predicting patient outcomes, leading to improved treatments and care.

Improved Safety: Machine learning is used in autonomous vehicles to recognize and respond to their environment, reducing accidents and making transportation safer.

Challenges of Machine Learning:

Automation: Machine learning allows computers to automate tasks that would be time-consuming or challenging for humans. This leads to increased efficiency and productivity in various industries.

Accurate Predictions: Machine learning models can analyze vast amounts of data and make predictions with high accuracy. This helps in making informed decisions and solving complex problems more effectively.

Personalization: Machine learning enables personalized experiences for users. It powers recommendation systems in streaming platforms, online shopping, and social media, tailoring content and suggestions to individual preferences.

Medical Advancements: In the healthcare field, machine learning helps in diagnosing diseases, identifying patterns in medical images, and predicting patient outcomes, leading to improved treatments and care.

Improved Safety: Machine learning is used in autonomous vehicles to recognize and respond to their environment, reducing accidents and making transportation safer.

Module 2: Machine Learning Basics

What is an Algorithms of Machine Language

"An algorithm is like a set of step-by-step instructions for solving a problem. Imagine it as a recipe for making your favorite dish. Just like you follow the recipe to make the food, a computer follows the algorithm to solve a task. Algorithms help computers think and do things in an organized way, like finding the best route on a map or playing a game."

Types of Algorithims

Sorting Algorithms: These algorithms arrange a list of items in a specific order, such as numerical order or alphabetical order. Examples include Bubble Sort, Selection Sort, and Merge Sort.

Searching Algorithms: These algorithms look for a specific item within a collection of data. Examples include Linear Search and Binary Search.

Graph Algorithms: These algorithms work with interconnected data structures called graphs. They help find paths, distances, or other relationships between nodes in the graph. Examples include Depth-First Search (DFS) and Breadth-First Search (BFS).

Greedy Algorithms: These algorithms make locally optimal choices at each step to find an overall solution. They don't always guarantee the best solution, but they can be efficient for some problems. Examples include the Greedy Knapsack Algorithm.

Dynamic Programming: This is a technique used to solve complex problems by breaking them down into smaller subproblems and storing their solutions to avoid redundant calculations.

Divide and Conquer Algorithms: These algorithms divide a problem into smaller, more manageable parts, solve each part separately, and then combine the solutions to get the final result. Examples include Quick Sort and Merge Sort.

Module 2: Machine Learning Basics

What is an Algorithms of Machine Language

Sorting Algorithms: These algorithms arrange a list of items in a specific order, such as numerical order or alphabetical order. Examples include Bubble Sort, Selection Sort, and Merge Sort.

Searching Algorithms: These algorithms look for a specific item within a collection of data. Examples include Linear Search and Binary Search.

Graph Algorithms: These algorithms work with interconnected data structures called graphs. They help find paths, distances, or other relationships between nodes in the graph. Examples include Depth-First Search (DFS) and Breadth-First Search (BFS).

Greedy Algorithms: These algorithms make locally optimal choices at each step to find an overall solution. They don't always guarantee the best solution, but they can be efficient for some problems. Examples include the Greedy Knapsack Algorithm.

Dynamic Programming: This is a technique used to solve complex problems by breaking them down into smaller subproblems and storing their solutions to avoid redundant calculations.

Divide and Conquer Algorithms: These algorithms divide a problem into smaller, more manageable parts, solve each part separately, and then combine the solutions to get the final result. Examples include Quick Sort and Merge Sort.

Module 2: Machine Learning Basics

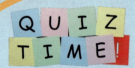

Machine Learning Basics

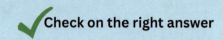 Check on the right answer

1. What is machine learning?

	a) Teaching computers to learn from data
	b) Writing code to control robots
	c) Designing new computer hardware

2. Which type of machine learning uses labeled data for training?

	a) Unsupervised learning
	b) Reinforcement learning
	c) Supervised learning

3. Which machine learning type is best for exploring patterns in data without labeled examples?

	a) Unsupervised learning
	b) Reinforcement learning
	c) Supervised learning

Module 2: Machine Learning Basics

Machine Learning Basics

✓ Check on the right answer

4. What are some real-life examples of machine learning applications?

	a) Sorting emails, diagnosing diseases, and autonomous vehicles
	b) Playing games, writing essays, and cooking recipes
	c) Sending emails, playing music, and drawing pictures

5. Which machine learning technique helps computers understand human language better?

	a) Natural Language Processing (NLP)
	b) Image Recognition
	c) Speech Synthesis

6. What does the term "bias" refer to in machine learning?

	a) The tendency of computers to learn quickly
	b) Unfair treatment based on personal opinions
	c) Unintended discrimination in data or algorithms

Module 2: Machine Learning Basics

Machine Learning Basics

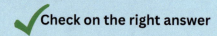 Check on the right answer

7. How do machine learning models improve over time?

	a) By getting smarter without any training
	b) By making more mistakes and learning from them
	c) By memorizing the training data exactly

8. Which machine learning algorithm is used for both regression and classification tasks?

	a) Decision tree
	b) Linear regression
	c) K-nearest neighbors (KNN)

9. What is the main goal of unsupervised learning?

	a) To predict future outcomes based on historical data
	b) To explore patterns and relationships in data without labeled examples
	c) To classify data into specific categories

Module 3:
Natural Language Processing (NLP)

Module 3: Natural Language Processing

Introduction to Natural Language Processing (NLP)

Natural Language Processing, commonly abbreviated as NLP, is a branch of artificial intelligence that focuses on the interaction between computers and human language. The primary goal of NLP is to enable machines to understand, interpret, and generate human language in a way that is both meaningful and contextually relevant.

Natural Language Processing, or NLP for short, is like teaching computers to understand and talk to us, just like we talk to each other. It's a cool part of computer science and helps us use technology in a smarter way.

Key Concepts in NLP

Tokenization: The process of breaking down text into individual units, or tokens, such as words or subwords. Tokenization is a fundamental step in NLP as it prepares the text for further analysis.

Part-of-Speech (POS) Tagging: Assigning grammatical labels to words in a sentence, such as nouns, verbs, adjectives, etc. POS tagging helps in understanding the syntactic structure of a sentence.

Named Entity Recognition (NER): Identifying and classifying named entities (e.g., names of people, places, organizations) in a text.

Sentiment Analysis: Determining the sentiment or emotion expressed in a piece of text, whether positive, negative, or neutral.

Machine Translation: Automatically translating text from one language to another.

Speech Recognition: Converting spoken language into written text.

Text Generation: Creating human-like text based on given prompts or contexts.

Module 3: Natural Language Processing

Understanding NLP at a Glance

1. Segmentation

Segmentation is the process of dividing a larger entity into smaller, manageable parts. Like 'NHL or National Hockey League, is a popular hockey league in North America'. It can broken down as:
NHL or National Hockey League,
is a popular hockey league in North America

2. Tokenization

Tokenization is like chopping a sentence into individual words. Imagine taking a sentence like
"I love reading books" and splitting it into four pieces:

"I,"
"love,"
"reading,"
and "books."

3. Stop Words

Stop words are like traffic signs for the computer. They're common words like "the," "and," "is," or "in" that don't carry a lot of meaning on their own. We often remove them because they can clutter up our analysis, like taking out unimportant road signs to focus on the important ones.

4. Stemming

Stemming is like finding the root of a word. For example, if you have the words "jumping," "jumps," and "jumped," stemming turns them into the base word "jump." It helps the computer group similar words together.

Understanding NLP at a Glance

5. Lemmatization

Lemmatization is like finding the dictionary form of a word. Instead of just getting "jump," you might also get "jumped" turned into "jump." It's like making sure all the words are in their official, original form.

6. Speech Tagging:

Speech tagging is like putting labels on words to show their roles in a sentence. For instance, it helps the computer know that "run" can be a verb ("I run") or a noun ("I had a run"). It's like telling the computer the job each word is doing.

7. Named Entity Tagging

Named Entity Tagging is like playing detective with names. It helps the computer find names of people, places, organizations, and more in a text. So, if you're reading about "New York City," the computer knows that's a place.

NLP encompasses a wide range of methods and tools used to enable computers to understand, interpret, and work with human language. These techniques are essential components of NLP that help computers process and analyze text data more effectively. NLP plays a crucial role in various applications, including chatbots, language translation, sentiment analysis, search engines, and much more. It's all about making computers smarter when it comes to understanding and working with human languages.

Module 3: Natural Language Processing

How Natural Language Processing (NLP) Works

Understanding Human Language: NLP is like teaching computers to understand how we talk and write, just like when we communicate with our friends or family.

Breaking Down Words: NLP starts by breaking down sentences and words into smaller pieces. These smaller pieces are like puzzle blocks that the computer can work with.

Parts of Speech: NLP figures out what role each word plays in a sentence. It's like a game of assigning jobs! For example, it knows which words are nouns (names of people, places, or things), verbs (action words), adjectives (describing words), and so on.

Finding Meaning: Once NLP knows the parts of speech, it can understand the meaning of sentences better. It's like putting the puzzle pieces together to see the whole picture.

Handling Ambiguity: Sometimes, words can have different meanings depending on the context. NLP tries its best to understand the right meaning by looking at the other words around it.

Sentiment Analysis: NLP can even guess how someone feels based on what they write or say. It can tell if someone is happy, sad, or neutral by looking at the words they use.

Using Past Knowledge: NLP learns from lots of examples to get better at understanding language. Just like how we learn from reading and talking to others, NLP learns from reading lots of text.

Module 3: Natural Language Processing

Making Language Models: NLP creates language models, which are like smart dictionaries. These models help computers predict what words or sentences might come next.

Making Our Devices Smarter: NLP is used in things like voice assistants (like Siri or Google Assistant) and chatbots. They use NLP to understand our questions and give us helpful answers.

Language Translation: NLP also helps in translating languages. It can change words from one language to another so we can understand people from different countries.

Improving Every Day: NLP is always learning and getting better. As more people use it, NLP becomes even smarter at understanding and talking with us.

Conclusion

Natural Language Processing (NLP) is a smart way of making computers understand human language. It breaks down sentences, figures out the meanings, and even guesses how people feel! NLP is used in voice assistants, chatbots, language translation, and many other cool things. The more we use NLP, the better it gets at understanding us and making our devices even smarter!

Module 3: Natural Language Processing

NLP Applications in our Daily Life

Natural Language Processing (NLP) has numerous applications in our daily lives, such as:

- **Email Filtering:** NLP helps in filtering spam emails from our inbox. It can analyze the content of emails and identify patterns that are common in spam messages, keeping our inbox clean and organized.

- **Autocorrect and Predictive Text**: When we type on our smartphones, NLP suggests words and corrects our spelling mistakes. It predicts the next word we might type, making typing faster and more accurate.

- **Voice Search:** NLP powers voice search on our smartphones and other devices. We can ask questions out loud, and the device understands what we want and provides relevant answers.

- **Social Media Sentiment Analysis:** NLP is used to analyze social media posts and comments to understand how people feel about a particular topic, product, or event. Companies use this information to improve their products and services.

- **Search Engines:** When we type a question or phrase into a search engine like Google, NLP helps it understand our query and fetch relevant search results.

- **Text Summarization:** NLP can summarize long articles or documents, extracting the most important information and presenting it in a concise form.

- **Grammar Checking:** NLP is used in grammar checking tools to identify grammar and punctuation errors in our writing, helping us improve our writing skills.

Tokenization

Tokenization is the first step in Natural Language Processing (NLP) and involves breaking down a piece of text into smaller units called tokens. These tokens can be words, subwords, or even characters, depending on the specific task. The process of tokenization makes it easier for computers to process and understand the text. Instead of dealing with the entire text as a single block, tokenization breaks it down into manageable chunks.

In English, tokenization is typically done by splitting the text at spaces and punctuation marks. For example, the sentence "The quick brown fox jumps over the lazy dog" would be tokenized into individual words: ["The", "quick", "brown", "fox", "jumps", "over", "the", "lazy", "dog"].

Tokenization is essential because it provides the basic units that other NLP techniques can work with. For instance, it allows us to count the frequency of words, analyze their positions in sentences, or extract specific information from the text.

Moreover, tokenization is crucial for many NLP tasks like part-of-speech tagging, named entity recognition, and text classification. Tokenization becomes more complex when dealing with languages that don't use spaces, like Chinese or Japanese, or when handling emoticons, hashtags, or URLs in social media text.

Technique of NLP   **Module 3: Natural Language Processing**

Tokenization

There are several types of tokenization techniques used in Natural Language Processing (NLP), depending on the specific requirements of the task and the characteristics of the language being processed.
Here are some common types of tokenization:

1. Word Tokenization: This is the most basic form of tokenization, where the text is split into individual words. It works well for languages like English, where words are usually separated by spaces.

2. Sentence Tokenization: In this type, the text is split into individual sentences. It's useful when you want to analyze or process text on a sentence-by-sentence basis.

3. Subword Tokenization: Instead of breaking text into whole words, subword tokenization splits words into smaller units, such as subwords or characters. This is particularly helpful for languages with complex word structures or for handling rare or out-of-vocabulary words.

4. Byte-Pair Encoding (BPE): BPE is a type of subword tokenization that repeatedly merges the most frequently occurring character pairs to create subword units. It is commonly used in language modeling and machine translation tasks.

5. SentencePiece: Similar to BPE, SentencePiece is an unsupervised text tokenizer and detokenizer mainly used in neural network-based NLP tasks.

6. Regular Expression Tokenization: This technique uses predefined rules or regular expressions to split text into tokens based on specific patterns.

7. Treebank Tokenization: Treebank tokenization involves using tokenization guidelines from treebanks, which are collections of parsed sentences, often used in language corpora.

Tokenization

8. Rule-based Tokenization: In rule-based tokenization, specific rules are applied to determine how to split the text into tokens. This allows customization for domain-specific or language-specific tokenization requirements.

9. Named Entity Tokenization: For named entity recognition tasks, specialized tokenization techniques may be used to ensure that named entities are treated as separate tokens.

Each type of tokenization has its advantages and is selected based on the specific NLP task, the language characteristics, and the data being processed. Using the appropriate tokenization method is crucial to ensure accurate and meaningful NLP analysis.

Technique of NLP Module 3: Natural Language Processing

Part-of-Speech (POS) Tagging

Part-of-Speech (POS) tagging is a crucial Natural Language Processing (NLP) technique that involves assigning grammatical tags to each word in a sentence. These tags represent the syntactic category or the part of speech of each word, such as nouns, verbs, adjectives, adverbs, pronouns, prepositions, conjunctions, and more. POS tagging plays a vital role in understanding the structure and meaning of a sentence, enabling computers to grasp the relationships between words and the overall context.

Let's take a simple sentence and illustrate how Part-of-Speech (POS) tagging works:

Sentence: "The quick brown fox jumps over the lazy dog."

POS Tagging:

"The" -> Determiner (DET)
"quick" -> Adjective (ADJ)
"brown" -> Adjective (ADJ)
"fox" -> Noun (NOUN)
"jumps" -> Verb (VERB)
"over" -> Preposition (ADP)
"the" -> Determiner (DET)
"lazy" -> Adjective (ADJ)
"dog" -> Noun (NOUN)
"." -> Punctuation (PUNCT)

In this example, each word in the sentence is assigned a Part-of-Speech (POS) tag that represents its grammatical category. The POS tagging helps to understand the syntactic structure of the sentence and the role that each word plays.

Part-of-Speech (POS) Tagging

Part-of-Speech (POS) tagging is a crucial Natural Language Processing (NLP) technique that involves assigning grammatical tags to each word in a sentence. These tags represent the syntactic category or the part of speech of each word, such as nouns, verbs, adjectives, adverbs, pronouns, prepositions, conjunctions, and more. POS tagging plays a vital role in understanding the structure and meaning of a sentence, enabling computers to grasp the relationships between words and the overall context.

Let's take a simple sentence and illustrate how Part-of-Speech (POS) tagging works:

Sentence: "The quick brown fox jumps over the lazy dog."

POS Tagging:

"The" -> Determiner (DET)
"quick" -> Adjective (ADJ)
"brown" -> Adjective (ADJ)
"fox" -> Noun (NOUN)
"jumps" -> Verb (VERB)
"over" -> Preposition (ADP)
"the" -> Determiner (DET)
"lazy" -> Adjective (ADJ)
"dog" -> Noun (NOUN)
"." -> Punctuation (PUNCT)

In this example, each word in the sentence is assigned a Part-of-Speech (POS) tag that represents its grammatical category. The POS tagging helps to understand the syntactic structure of the sentence and the role that each word plays.

Technique of NLP Module 3: Natural Language Processing

Part-of-Speech (POS) Tagging

The POS tagging process begins with tokenization, where the text is split into individual words. Once the words are tokenized, the next step is to assign the appropriate POS tag to each word. This is achieved through the use of statistical algorithms and machine learning techniques. Machine learning models are trained on large annotated datasets, where each word is manually labeled with its corresponding POS tag. These models then use the patterns and relationships learned from the training data to predict POS tags for unseen words in new sentences.

POS tagging has numerous applications in NLP. One common use case is in information retrieval and search engines, where POS tagging helps in understanding user queries and delivering more relevant search results. It also plays a significant role in text-to-speech synthesis, as knowing the POS of each word helps the system to generate natural and fluent speech.

Additionally, POS tagging is essential for many downstream NLP tasks, such as named entity recognition, sentiment analysis, and text classification. For instance, knowing the POS of words is critical in sentiment analysis to identify the sentiment-bearing words (adjectives) that convey emotions in a sentence.

However, POS tagging is not without its challenges. Some words may have multiple possible POS tags depending on the context, leading to ambiguity. For example, the word "bank" can be a noun (financial institution) or a verb (to tilt or incline). Dealing with such ambiguity requires more sophisticated algorithms and context-aware models.

In summary, POS tagging is a fundamental technique in NLP that provides valuable information about the grammatical structure of a sentence. Its accurate implementation enhances the understanding of language and enables a wide range of applications, making it an indispensable tool in modern language processing systems. Researchers continue to improve POS tagging algorithms, making them more accurate and efficient for various real-world NLP applications.

Technique of NLP

Module 3: Natural Language Processing

Named Entity Recognition (NER)

The named entity recognition (NER) is one of the most popular data preprocessing task. It involves the identification of key information in the text and classification into a set of predefined categories. An entity is basically the thing that is consistently talked about or refer to in the text.

Named Entity Recognition (NER) is a crucial Natural Language Processing (NLP) technique that focuses on identifying and classifying named entities in a piece of text. Named entities are words or phrases that refer to specific entities, such as names of people, places, organizations, dates, time expressions, monetary values, and more. NER plays a vital role in understanding the context and extracting valuable information from unstructured text data.

NER is just a two-step process, below are the two steps that are involved:

- Detecting the entities from the text
- Classifying them into different categories

Some of the categories that are the most important architecture in NER such that:

- **Person**
- **Organization**
- **Place/ location**

Other common tasks include classifying of the following:

- **date/time.**
- **expression**
- **Numeral measurement (money, percent, weight, etc)**
- **E-mail address**

Technique of NLP
Module 3: Natural Language Processing

NER Application in Daily Life

NER is essential for a wide range of applications. In information extraction tasks, NER helps to identify key pieces of information from large text corpora, enabling data analysts to organize and analyze data more efficiently. For example, in the healthcare domain, NER can be used to extract information about medical conditions, treatments, and patient names from medical records.

NER is also valuable in sentiment analysis and social media monitoring. By recognizing named entities, sentiment analysis tools can understand the opinions and attitudes expressed towards specific individuals, organizations, or products in social media posts and reviews.

In the realm of language translation, NER is used to handle named entities during the translation process. Translating named entities accurately is crucial for maintaining the context and meaning of the text.

These examples demonstrate how NER enhances various aspects of our daily lives, making technology more efficient, personalized, and user-friendly. NER helps computers understand the context and significance of named entities, enabling them to provide us with more relevant and meaningful information and services.

Technique of NLP
Module 3: Natural Language Processing

Sentiment Analysis

Sentiment analysis, also known as opinion mining, is a type of technology that helps computers understand and categorize people's feelings, attitudes, and opinions expressed in written text. It can determine whether a piece of text is positive, negative, or neutral in its sentiment

The sentiment analysis process typically starts with text preprocessing, including tokenization, stopword removal, and stemming or lemmatization. Next, machine learning algorithms or deep learning models are trained on labeled datasets, where each piece of text is associated with its corresponding sentiment label. These models learn patterns and relationships between words and their sentiment labels, enabling them to predict the sentiment of unseen text.

Sentiment analysis has a wide range of real-world applications. In social media monitoring, businesses can gauge public sentiment towards their products and services, enabling them to make informed decisions and respond to customer feedback promptly. Sentiment analysis is also valuable in brand monitoring, allowing companies to assess their brand perception and track changes in consumer sentiment over time.

Moreover, sentiment analysis is applied in market research to analyze customer feedback and reviews, providing valuable insights into consumer preferences, product improvements, and competitive intelligence. In the financial sector, sentiment analysis of news articles and social media content can influence investment decisions by assessing market sentiment.

Technique of NLP

Module 3: Natural Language Processing

Type of Sentiment Analysis

Sentiment analysis is the process of detecting positive or negative sentiment in text. It's often used by businesses to detect sentiment in social data, gauge brand reputation, and understand customers.

In Natural Language Processing (NLP), there are several types of sentiment analysis techniques used to understand and categorize the sentiment expressed in text. Some of the common types of sentiment analysis are:

Graded Sentiment Analysis
If polarity precision is important to your business, you might consider expanding your polarity categories to include different levels of positive and negative:

- **Very positive**
- **Positive**
- **Neutral**
- **Negative**
- **Very negative**

This is usually referred to as graded or fine-grained sentiment analysis, and could be used to interpret 5-star ratings in a review, for example:

- **Very Positive = 5 stars**
- **Very Negative = 1 star**

Technique of NLP

Module 3: Natural Language Processing

Type of Sentiment Analysis

Document-level Sentiment Analysis: This type of sentiment analysis focuses on determining the overall sentiment of an entire document or text. It classifies the entire piece of text as positive, negative, or neutral based on the sentiments expressed throughout the document.

Sentence-level Sentiment Analysis: In sentence-level sentiment analysis, each sentence in a document is analyzed individually to identify its sentiment. This allows for a more granular understanding of the emotions conveyed within each sentence.

Aspect-based Sentiment Analysis: Aspect-based sentiment analysis goes beyond determining overall sentiment and focuses on extracting sentiment towards specific aspects or features of a product, service, or topic. It helps in understanding how people feel about different aspects mentioned in the text.

Entity-level Sentiment Analysis: Entity-level sentiment analysis involves identifying and analyzing sentiment towards named entities, such as people, places, organizations, or products mentioned in the text. It helps in understanding sentiments related to specific entities.

Comparative Sentiment Analysis: Comparative sentiment analysis compares the sentiment between different entities or aspects. It determines which entity or aspect is more positively or negatively perceived compared to others.

Multilingual Sentiment Analysis: Multilingual sentiment analysis deals with analyzing sentiments expressed in multiple languages. It allows for sentiment analysis on a global scale, considering the diversity of languages used in different regions.

Sarcasm and Irony Detection: Sarcasm and irony detection is a challenging aspect of sentiment analysis, as it requires identifying instances where the text expresses the opposite of its literal meaning.

Technique of NLP

Module 3: Natural Language Processing

Machine Translation

"If you talk to a man in a language he understands, that goes to his head. If you talk to him in his own language, that goes to his heart."
– Nelson Mandela

Machine translation is a cutting-edge application of Natural Language Processing (NLP) that aims to automatically translate text or speech from one language to another. By leveraging advanced algorithms and neural networks, machine translation breaks down language barriers, enabling effective communication and cross-cultural exchange on a global scale. From online translation services to language learning apps, machine translation plays a vital role in bridging linguistic gaps and fostering global connectivity.

The process of machine translation involves complex algorithms and models that analyze the structure and meaning of sentences in the source language and generate corresponding sentences in the target language. There are two main approaches to machine translation: rule-based and statistical (data-driven) methods. In rule-based translation, linguistic rules and dictionaries are used to perform the translation. Statistical machine translation, on the other hand, relies on vast amounts of bilingual text data to build probabilistic models that predict the best translations based on statistical patterns.

With the rise of deep learning, neural machine translation (NMT) has emerged as a state-of-the-art approach in machine translation. NMT uses neural networks, particularly sequence-to-sequence models with attention mechanisms, to learn the mapping between source and target languages. NMT has shown significant improvements in translation quality, producing more fluent and contextually accurate translations compared to traditional statistical methods.

Technique of NLP

Module 3: Natural Language Processing

Types of Machine Translation

There are several types of machine translation approaches available, each with its own strengths and limitations. Here are some of the main types of machine translation:

Rule-Based Machine Translation (RBMT): RBMT relies on linguistic rules and dictionaries to perform translations. Linguists manually create these rules, specifying how words and phrases in the source language should be translated into the target language. While rule-based systems can handle some grammar and syntax complexities, they often struggle with idiomatic expressions and may not scale well for languages with many exceptions.

Statistical Machine Translation (SMT): SMT uses statistical models based on large bilingual corpora to determine the best translations. These models learn from vast amounts of data and identify patterns and relationships between words and phrases in different languages. SMT has been widely used and can handle a range of language pairs, but it may produce translations that lack fluency and coherence.

Neural Machine Translation (NMT): NMT is a modern approach that employs deep learning neural networks, specifically sequence-to-sequence models with attention mechanisms. NMT learns to map the source language to the target language by processing entire sentences as opposed to individual words. NMT has significantly improved translation quality, producing more fluent and contextually accurate translations compared to older methods.

Hybrid Machine Translation: Hybrid machine translation combines multiple approaches, such as rule-based and statistical or statistical and neural, to leverage the strengths of each. These systems attempt to overcome the limitations of individual methods and provide more accurate translations.

Technique of NLP

Module 3: Natural Language Processing

Speech Recognition

Speech recognition is an amazing technology that allows computers to understand spoken words and convert them into written text.

NLP and Voice Recognition are complementary but different. Voice Recognition focuses on processing voice data to convert it into a structured form such as text. NLP focuses on understanding the meaning by processing text input. Voice Recognition can work without NLP, but NLP cannot directly process audio inputs

Speech recognition is an exciting technology that allows computers to understand and interpret human speech. Just like how we use our ears to listen and understand what others say, speech recognition enables computers to "listen" to spoken words and convert them into written text. This incredible technology makes it easier for us to interact with computers and devices using our voice, making tasks like sending messages, searching the web, and setting reminders more convenient.

Speech recognition systems work through a series of complex algorithms and models. When we speak into a microphone or use a voice assistant on our devices, the speech recognition software breaks down our speech into smaller units, such as individual sounds and words. It then matches these units with patterns it has learned from vast amounts of recorded speech data during its training.

For example, when we say "Hello, how are you?", the speech recognition system processes the sound waves and identifies each word. It then converts the spoken words into written text, displaying "Hello, how are you?" on the screen.

Technique of NLP

Module 3: Natural Language Processing

Speech Recognition

Speech recognition is used in various everyday applications that we might already be familiar with. Virtual assistants like Siri, Google Assistant, and Alexa are popular examples of speech recognition technology. They can answer questions, provide weather updates, play music, and even control smart home devices—all by listening to our voice commands.

Speech recognition also finds applications in accessibility tools for people with disabilities. It allows individuals who have difficulty typing or using a keyboard to control computers and interact with technology using their voices.

While speech recognition is incredibly useful, it's not always perfect. Sometimes, it may misinterpret words, especially if there is background noise or if someone speaks quickly. However, continuous research and advancements in technology are steadily improving speech recognition accuracy.

In conclusion, speech recognition is a remarkable technology that enables computers to understand and respond to our spoken words. It has transformed the way we interact with technology and has made tasks more accessible and efficient. As speech recognition technology continues to evolve, it promises to play an even more significant role in our daily lives, making voice interactions with computers and devices an integral part of our future.

Technique of NLP

Types of Speech Recognition

- **Connected word system**
  The combination of two words forms a one single word. The minimal pause is taken between the utterance of two words and isolated word is formed.
- **Continuous speech recognizer**
  It is also known as computer dictation. It is natural speech of a speaker.
- **Spontaneous speech system**
  The natural sounds like "ums" "aah" "hmm" utterance along with speech.
- **Voice verification/identification**
  The identification and verification of specific speaker's voice by applying various tools and techniques.

Technique of NLP

Module 3: Natural Language Processing

Speech Recognition in our Daily Life

Speech recognition has become increasingly prevalent in our daily lives, revolutionizing the way we interact with technology and making tasks more convenient and accessible. Here are some examples of speech recognition in daily life:

Virtual Assistants: Popular virtual assistants like Siri (Apple), Google Assistant (Google), Alexa (Amazon), and Cortana (Microsoft) use speech recognition to understand and respond to voice commands. They can answer questions, set reminders, play music, control smart home devices, and perform various tasks based on spoken instructions.

Voice Search: Voice search is widely used in search engines like Google and Bing. By speaking their queries, users can find information, get directions, or look up facts without typing on a keyboard.

In-Car Systems: Many modern vehicles come equipped with voice-activated infotainment systems. Drivers can use speech recognition to make hands-free calls, control the audio system, get directions, or access other car features.

Smart Home Devices: Devices like smart speakers and smart displays use speech recognition to respond to voice commands for tasks like turning on lights, adjusting thermostats, setting timers, and playing media.

Language Translation Apps: Some language translation apps use speech recognition to facilitate real-time translation. Users can speak in one language, and the app translates their speech into another language, making it easier to communicate in foreign countries.

Technique of NLP

Module 3: Natural Language Processing

Text Generation

Text generation is a process where an AI system produces written content, imitating human language patterns and styles. The process involves generating coherent and meaningful text that resembles natural human communication.

Text generation is a fascinating aspect of Natural Language Processing (NLP) that allows computers to create written text, just like humans do! It's like having a virtual writer that can compose stories, poems, and even conversations. Text generation in NLP uses sophisticated algorithms and models to understand language patterns and produce coherent and meaningful sentences.

One popular technique for text generation is called "language modeling." Imagine you have a friend who knows a lot about books and can predict what words or phrases might come next in a story. Language models work in a similar way; they learn from vast collections of written text, like books and articles, to predict the next word in a sentence based on the words that came before it. This enables the model to generate new sentences that sound natural and logical.

Text generation is used in various applications. For instance, you might have heard of chatbots - virtual assistants that can have conversations with people. Chatbots use text generation to respond to our messages by understanding the context and generating appropriate replies. They can help answer questions, provide information, or engage in small talk.

Technique of NLP

Text Generation

Another exciting application is in creative writing. Text generation models have been used to create stories, poems, and even song lyrics! It's like having an AI co-author who can come up with new and imaginative ideas.

However, text generation is not without its challenges. Sometimes, the generated text may not make complete sense or could be misleading. This is because language can be ambiguous, and computers may not fully understand the context or emotions behind the words.

Researchers are continually working to improve text generation algorithms, making them more accurate and human-like. As you can imagine, this field of NLP opens up a world of possibilities. Computers can learn to imitate different writing styles, generate personalized content, and even help people who have difficulty expressing themselves in writing.

In conclusion, text generation is an exciting aspect of NLP that allows computers to create written text, much like human writers. Through language modeling and other sophisticated techniques, computers can generate stories, poems, and conversations. While challenges remain, text generation has promising applications in chatbots, creative writing, and assisting those who struggle with expressing themselves in writing. With further advancements in technology, text generation will undoubtedly continue to bring more creativity and versatility to the world of language processing.

Technique of NLP

Module 3: Natural Language Processing

Text Generation
How it Works

Text generators in NLP work using sophisticated algorithms and models that have been trained on vast amounts of textual data. The process of how a text generator works can be summarized in the following steps:

Data Collection and Preprocessing: To train a text generator, a large dataset of written text is collected from various sources, such as books, articles, and websites. The data is preprocessed by removing any irrelevant information, converting text to lowercase, and splitting it into sentences or smaller units.

Language Modeling: The core technique used in text generation is language modeling. Language models learn from the preprocessed data to understand the structure and patterns of language. They aim to predict the likelihood of the next word in a sentence based on the sequence of words that came before it. This is done using probabilistic methods and statistical analysis of the training data.

Generating Text: Once the language model is trained, it can be used to generate text. To do this, the text generator takes a starting word or phrase as input. The generator then predicts the most likely next word based on the language model's training. This process is repeated iteratively to generate a sequence of words, forming coherent sentences.

Diversity and Creativity: Text generators can be designed to be more creative by adding randomness or variability to the predictions. This randomness introduces diversity in the generated text, making it sound more human-like and less repetitive.

Post-Processing: After generating text, post-processing steps are applied to refine the output. This may involve filtering out inappropriate content, correcting grammar mistakes, or ensuring the generated text follows certain guidelines or constraints.

Evaluating and Fine-Tuning: Text generators are evaluated based on their ability to produce coherent and relevant text. If needed, the model can be fine-tuned by adjusting its parameters or training it on additional data to improve its performance.

Module 3: Natural Language Processing

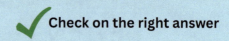 Check on the right answer

1. What does NLP stand for?

	a) Natural Linguistic Processing
	b) Neural Language Prediction
	c) Natural Language Processing

2. What is tokenization in NLP?

	a) The process of converting text into tokens for easy processing
	b) The process of converting speech to text
	c) The process of translating one language to another

3. Part-of-Speech (POS) Tagging

	a) To determine the sentiment of a piece of text
	b) To identify and classify named entities in text
	c) To assign grammatical tags to each word in a sentence

Module 3:
Natural Language Processing

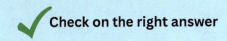
Check on the right answer

4. Named Entity Recognition (NER)

	a) Natural Entity Recognition
	b) Named Entity Relevance
	c) Named Entity Recognition

5. What does sentiment analysis in NLP focus on?

	a) Understanding the syntactic structure of a sentence
	b) Identifying and classifying named entities in a piece of text
	c) Analyzing and categorizing the emotions, attitudes, and opinions expressed in text

6. What are language models in NLP used for?

	a) Predicting the likelihood of a sequence of words in a sentence
	b) Identifying the parts of speech in a sentence
	c) Classifying named entities in text

Page: 72

Module 3: Natural Language Processing

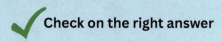 Check on the right answer

7. What is the main purpose of machine translation in NLP?

	a) Converting spoken words into written text
	b) Predicting the next word in a sentence
	c) Translating text from one language to another

8. What does text summarization in NLP involve?

	a) Breaking down text into smaller units called tokens
	b) Identifying and classifying named entities in a piece of text
	c) Generating a concise summary of a longer text while retaining important information

9. What does speech recognition in NLP refer to?

	a) Analyzing and categorizing emotions in spoken words
	b) Identifying and classifying named entities in speech
	c) Converting spoken words into written text

Module 4: Introduction to Computer Vision

Module 4: Introduction to Computer Vision

Introduction to Computer Vision

EXPLORING THE MAGICAL WORLD OF COMPUTER VISION

Imagine a world where computers can see and understand just like we do! Welcome to the fascinating realm of Computer Vision, a magical branch of computer science that enables machines to perceive and interpret the world through images and videos. It's like giving eyes to computers, and it opens up a world of exciting possibilities!

You see, just as our eyes capture the beauty of the world around us, computer vision allows computers to capture and analyze the visual information they receive. It's like teaching them to recognize shapes, colors, and even familiar faces. Just like you can identify a cat or a dog, computer vision can do the same! But instead of whiskers and wagging tails, it looks for patterns in the images and videos it "sees."

One of the most thrilling parts of computer vision is that it helps computers see things we might miss. For example, have you ever played a game where you have to find hidden objects in a picture? Computer vision can do that too! It can find tiny details, detect hidden patterns, and even spot the differences between two seemingly identical images. How cool is that?

Not only that, but computer vision also plays a crucial role in technology we use every day. Have you ever wondered how your phone can unlock just by scanning your face? That's computer vision in action! It recognizes your unique features and grants you access to your device. It's like having your phone recognize you like a friend!

So, are you ready to dive into this magical world of computer vision? Get ready to explore, learn, and be amazed by the incredible things computers can do with their newfound "eyes"! It's like bringing a touch of magic to our everyday lives!

Module 4: Introduction to Computer Vision

Fundamental Concepts in Computer Vision

Computer Vision aims to enable machines to interpret and make decisions based on visual data, much like humans do. At its core, it involves understanding and manipulating digital images and videos. Before delving into advanced algorithms and techniques, it's essential to grasp the foundational concepts that underlie all visual data processing. These fundamental ideas provide the groundwork for understanding how images are represented, how colors are organized, and how various mathematical operations can transform these images for further analysis.

Digital Image Representation:

Digital images are represented in a computer as a matrix of pixel values. Each pixel has a numerical value that corresponds to its brightness or color. For grayscale images, this is a single value (usually between 0 for black and 255 for white). For color images, typically in the RGB format, there are three values for each pixel, representing the Red, Green, and Blue channels. The combination of these values produces the full spectrum of colors. The resolution of an image is determined by its width and height in pixels.

Color Spaces

A color space is a specific way of organizing colors and can be thought of as a method to represent colors in a consistent format. The most common color space is RGB (Red, Green, Blue), but there are many others like HSV (Hue, Saturation, Value), YUV, and LAB. Each color space has its advantages depending on the application. For instance, the HSV space is often used in tasks where color and brightness are treated separately, as 'Value' represents brightness, while 'Hue' represents color.

Module 4: Introduction to Computer Vision

Fundamental Concepts in Computer Vision

Image Transforms

Image transforms are mathematical operations applied to images to convert them from one domain to another, often to extract certain features or characteristics. Common image transforms include the Fourier Transform, which converts an image from the spatial domain to the frequency domain, and the Wavelet Transform, which can decompose an image into different frequency components at different resolutions. These transforms are essential for tasks like image compression, noise reduction, and feature extraction.

These foundational concepts are the building blocks for more advanced techniques in computer vision, bridging the gap between raw pixel data and meaningful visual understanding.

Module 4: Introduction to Computer Vision

Computer Vision Techniques

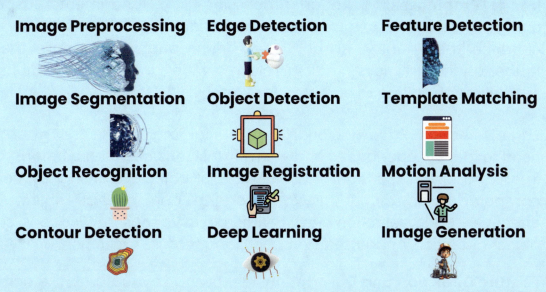

These techniques form the foundation of computer vision and are combined and adapted in various ways to solve specific problems and applications within the field. Advances in machine learning, especially deep learning, have significantly boosted the capabilities of computer vision systems in recent years, enabling them to achieve impressive levels of accuracy and performance in various tasks.

Computer Vision Techniques

Image Preprocessing: Image processing is a fundamental aspect of computer vision that involves manipulating and analyzing digital images to enhance their quality, extract useful information, or prepare them for further analysis. It plays a crucial role in a wide range of applications, from simple image editing to complex computer vision tasks.

Edge Detection: Edge detection is a crucial image processing technique used to identify boundaries and sharp transitions between different regions in an image. It helps highlight the edges of objects and shapes, enabling computer vision algorithms to recognize and analyze objects more effectively. Edge detection plays a vital role in various applications, such as object detection, image segmentation, and feature extraction.

Feature Detection and Description: Identifying key features, like corners or keypoints, and describing them in a way that can be used for recognition tasks. It involves identifying unique keypoints or distinctive patterns in an image to enable recognition and matching tasks in computer vision applications.

Image segmentation: This is the process of dividing an image into meaningful regions or segments to simplify its analysis. It helps isolate objects of interest, allowing computer vision algorithms to focus on specific areas and extract valuable information for tasks like object detection, tracking, and scene understanding.

Object detection: This is a vital computer vision task that involves locating and classifying objects within an image or video. It enables machines to recognize and understand their surroundings by identifying multiple objects simultaneously. Object detection finds applications in autonomous vehicles, surveillance, robotics, and various other fields that require real-time scene analysis.

Computer Vision Techniques

Template matching: This is an image processing technique used to locate a small template image within a larger image. It involves comparing the template's pixel values with those of overlapping regions in the larger image to find the best match. Template matching is useful in tasks like object localization and pattern recognition.

Object recognition: This is a computer vision task that involves identifying and classifying objects in images or videos. It goes beyond object detection by not only locating objects but also associating them with specific categories or labels. Deep learning-based methods, such as CNNs, have significantly improved object recognition accuracy, enabling applications like image tagging and content-based image retrieval.

Image registration: This is the process of aligning multiple images of the same scene or object taken from different viewpoints, times, or sensors. It ensures that the images are in the same coordinate system, enabling comparison and analysis. Image registration finds applications in medical imaging, remote sensing, and creating panoramic images by stitching together multiple photographs.

Motion analysis: This in computer vision involves studying and understanding the movement of objects or people within an image or video sequence. It includes tasks like motion tracking, estimating object trajectories, and recognizing human actions. Motion analysis finds applications in surveillance, sports analysis, autonomous navigation, and character animation in computer graphics.

Contour detection: This is an image processing technique that identifies and extracts the outlines or boundaries of objects in an image. It locates regions with significant changes in intensity, representing the edges of objects. Contour detection plays a crucial role in image segmentation, object recognition, and shape analysis in computer vision applications.

Module 4: Introduction to Computer Vision

Computer Vision Techniques

Deep learning: This is a subfield of artificial intelligence that utilizes deep neural networks to process and learn from vast amounts of data. It has revolutionized various domains, including computer vision, natural language processing, and speech recognition. Deep learning enables machines to achieve remarkable performance in complex tasks, surpassing traditional methods in many areas.

Image generation: This is a fascinating application of deep learning where computer models, such as Generative Adversarial Networks (GANs), create new images from scratch. These models learn from existing data and generate realistic, high-quality images that resemble real-world examples. Image generation finds applications in art, design, data augmentation, and content creation.

Module 4: Introduction to Computer Vision

Computer Vision in our Daily Life

Computer vision is increasingly integrated into various aspects of our daily lives. Here are five examples of how computer vision is used in everyday scenarios:

Face Unlock on Smartphones: Many smartphones now use computer vision algorithms to unlock the device by recognizing the user's face. The front-facing camera captures and analyzes facial features to grant access securely.

Social Media Filters and AR Effects: Apps like Instagram and Snapchat use computer vision to apply fun filters and augmented reality (AR) effects to our selfies, transforming our appearance and adding entertaining elements.

Automated Checkout in Stores: Some stores have implemented computer vision-based checkout systems. Customers can pick up items, and cameras equipped with computer vision technology automatically detect the products they've chosen, tally up the total, and charge the customer's account.

Traffic Surveillance and Monitoring: Computer vision is used in traffic cameras and surveillance systems to monitor traffic flow, detect traffic violations, and manage traffic signals efficiently.

Medical Imaging and Diagnostics: In the medical field, computer vision is employed to analyze medical images like X-rays, MRIs, and CT scans, assisting doctors in diagnosing diseases and conditions more accurately.

Module 4: Introduction to Computer Vision

How Does Computer Vision Work?

The basis for much computer vision work is 2D images, as shown below. While images may seem like a complex input, we can decompose them into raw numbers. Images are really just a combination of individual pixels and each pixel can be represented by a number (grayscale) or combination of numbers such as (255, 0, 0—<u>RGB</u>).

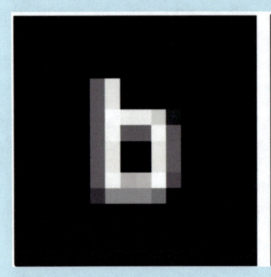
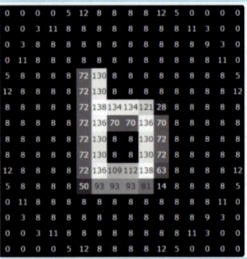

Once we've translated an image to a set of numbers, a computer vision algorithm applies processing. One way to do this is a classic technique called convolutional neural networks (CNNs) that uses layers to group together the pixels in order to create successively more meaningful representations of the data. A CNN may first translate pixels into lines, which are then combined to form features such as eyes and finally combined to create more complex items such as face shapes.

Module 4: Introduction to Computer Vision

Processing Steps of Computer Vision

Image Acquisition

This is the first step where a digital image or video is captured using devices like cameras, satellites, or scanners. Quality and clarity of acquired images directly impact the accuracy of subsequent computer vision tasks. Proper lighting, resolution, and focus are crucial here.

Pre-processing

Before analysis, images often undergo various processing steps to enhance quality and remove noise. This includes grayscale conversion, histogram equalization, noise reduction, and normalization. Pre-processing ensures that the image is in the best possible form for feature extraction, making subsequent steps more effective.

Feature Extraction

This step involves identifying and extracting significant patterns or features from the image that are essential for further processing. Methods like edge detection, key point detection, and texture analysis are used in this step. Extracted features act as the input for algorithms, determining objects, patterns, or other relevant information in the image.

Segmentation

Segmentation divides an image into multiple segments or regions, each corresponding to different objects or parts of objects. It simplifies the image analysis by breaking it down into meaningful parts, making object recognition and scene understanding more manageable.

Recognition and Interpretation

The system identifies objects or patterns from the segmented image based on the extracted features. This step is crucial for tasks like object detection, facial recognition, and more, allowing the system to "understand" the content of the image.

Processing Steps of Computer Vision

Post-processing

After recognition, results are furthered refined or processed to enhance accuracy or clarity. This involves removing false positives, refining object boundaries, or applying additional filters. Ensures the final output is as accurate and clear as possible, optimizing the results of the computer vision task.

Action or Output

Based on the interpreted data, the system might produce an output or perform an action. for example, this could be displaying the name of a recognized face, triggering an alert for a security camera when unauthorized movement is detected, or providing a diagnosis in medical imaging.

Importance

This is the end goal of most computer vision systems, translating the visual data into meaningful, actionable insights or results.

In essence, computer vision seeks to replicate the capabilities of human vision by automatically interpreting and making decisions based on visual data. The process involves a series of steps, from capturing the image to producing a final output or action, each crucial for the system's overall effectiveness.

Module 4: Introduction to Computer Vision

Computer Vision

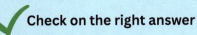 Check on the right answer

1. What is computer vision?

	a) Giving computers the ability to see and understand images and videos.
	b) Allowing computers to perform mathematical calculations.
	c) Enabling computers to play video games.

2. What is the purpose of image segmentation in computer vision?

	a) Enhancing image resolution.
	b) Allowing computers to perform mathematical calculations.
	b) Dividing an image into meaningful regions or segments.

3. Which computer vision technique is used to detect emotions on human faces?

	a) Image Super-Resolution.
	b) Feature Detection.
	c) Emotion Recognition.

Module 4: Introduction to Computer Vision

Computer Vision

✓ Check on the right answer

4. What does object detection in computer vision involve?

	a) Locating and classifying objects in images or videos.
	b) Enhancing the brightness and contrast of images.
	c) Removing noise from images.

5. How does image blurring help in computer vision?

	a) It enhances image resolution.
	b) It reduces the sharpness of image details.
	c) It adds more colors to the image.

6. Which technique in computer vision is used to align multiple images taken from different viewpoints?

	a) Image Restoration.
	b) Image Registration.
	c) Image Compression.

Module 4: Introduction to Computer Vision

Computer Vision

✓ Check on the right answer

7. What is the purpose of feature detection in computer vision?

	a) Identifying unique keypoints or patterns in an image.
	b) Enhancing the brightness and contrast of images.
	c) Enhancing image quality.

8. What task does motion analysis perform in computer vision?

	a) Analyzing the colors in an image.
	b) Identifying and understanding object movement in a video.
	c) Removing noise from images.

9. What is the role of deep learning in computer vision?

	a) Enhancing image resolution.
	b) Using deep neural networks for complex tasks.
	c) Applying filters to images

Module 5:
Introduction to Robotics

Module 4: Introduction to Computer Vision

Introduction to Robotics

Robotics is an exciting field of technology that deals with designing, building, and programming machines called robots. These robots are not just ordinary machines; they are smart and can perform tasks on their own with little or no human intervention. Imagine having a helpful companion by your side, like a friend who can follow instructions and complete tasks to make your life easier and more enjoyable. That's what robots are!

Robots have found their way into various aspects of our daily lives and have become an integral part of many industries. Let's explore some fascinating real-life applications of robotics:

Manufacturing Robots: In factories and production lines, you'll find robots tirelessly assembling cars, electronics, and other products. They work with great precision, speed, and accuracy, making our favorite gadgets and vehicles.

Medical Robots: Robots are revolutionizing healthcare by assisting doctors in surgeries, allowing for precise movements and reducing risks. Some robots can even deliver medicines and perform routine tasks in hospitals.

Agricultural Robots: In the field of agriculture, robots are helping farmers in planting, watering, and harvesting crops. They can work for long hours and handle repetitive tasks, freeing up farmers to focus on other essential activities.

Module 5: Introduction to Robotics

Introduction to Robotics

Exploration Robots: Ever wondered how we explore distant planets like Mars? Well, we send robots there! These robots, called rovers, are like scientific explorers on wheels, helping scientists learn more about the universe.

Service Robots: Have you seen robots cleaning the floor or delivering packages? These robots are designed to assist us in our homes and offices, making our living spaces cleaner and more organized.

Educational Robots: Some robots are specially created to help students learn and understand complex subjects like math and science. They can be fun and interactive, making learning an enjoyable experience.

Entertainment Robots: Robots aren't all about work; they can be fun too! You might have seen robotic toys, pet-like robots, or even robots used in theme parks to entertain visitors.

Search and Rescue Robots: During emergencies like earthquakes or disasters, robots can enter dangerous areas to search for survivors and help rescue teams.

Robotics is a rapidly evolving field, and as technology advances, robots will continue to play an even more significant role in our lives. From everyday tasks to exploring the frontiers of space, robots are here to stay, making the world a better place for all of us. As you learn more about robotics, you'll be amazed at the endless possibilities and the fantastic future that lies ahead. Who knows, you might become a robotics engineer and create the next generation of innovative robots!

Module 5: Introduction to Robotics

Parts of Robots

Robots are complex machines, and just like any other machine, they are made up of several important parts that work together to make them function. Let's explore the essential components of a robot:

Sensors:

Sensors act as the robot's eyes, ears, and touch. They gather information from the robot's surroundings.
Examples of sensors include cameras for vision, microphones for hearing, and touch sensors to feel objects.

Actuators:

Actuators are like the muscles of a robot. They are responsible for moving the robot's different parts.
Motors and servos are common types of actuators that enable a robot's arms, legs, or wheels to move.

Controllers:

Controllers act as the robot's brain. They process information from the sensors and decide how the robot should respond.
Microcontrollers or computer chips are used as controllers to make decisions and control the robot's actions.

Module 5: Introduction to Robotics

Parts of Robots

Power Source:

Robots need energy to function, just like we need food to move. A power source provides the necessary energy to run the robot.
Batteries or rechargeable cells are commonly used as power sources in robots.

End Effectors:

End effectors are tools or attachments at the end of a robot's arm or manipulator. They allow the robot to interact with its environment.
Examples of end effectors are grippers for picking up objects, welding tools for industrial robots, or surgical instruments for medical robots.

Chassis or Body:

The chassis or body is the main framework of the robot. It holds all the other components together and provides structure and stability.
Depending on the type of robot, the chassis can vary, such as wheels for a mobile robot or arms and joints for a humanoid robot.

Communication Interface:

Robots often need to communicate with humans or other machines. Communication interfaces allow them to send and receive information.
Displays, speakers, or even computer screens can be used for communication

Module 5: Introduction to Robotics

Parts of Robots

Programming Interface:

Robots need instructions on how to perform tasks. A programming interface allows humans to write code or give commands to the robot.
It could be a physical panel with buttons or a software interface on a computer.

Safety Features:

Safety is crucial when dealing with robots, especially those working around humans. Safety features are mechanisms to prevent accidents and injuries. Sensors like proximity sensors can detect obstacles and stop the robot to avoid collisions.

Understanding these essential parts of a robot will help you grasp how these machines work and how different components come together to perform a wide range of tasks. Robotics is an exciting field with endless possibilities, and learning about these components is just the beginning of an incredible journey into the world of technology and automation.

Module 5: Introduction to Robotics

Types of Robots

Robots come in various shapes and sizes, each designed to perform specific tasks based on their unique features and capabilities. Let's explore some fascinating types of robots:

Industrial Robots:

Industrial robots are commonly found in factories and manufacturing plants. They are strong, precise, and can handle heavy-duty tasks.
These robots are programmed to perform repetitive jobs like welding, painting, assembling, and packaging items on production lines.
Industrial robots are essential in making the manufacturing process faster, more efficient, and safer for human workers.

Service Robots:

Service robots are designed to assist and help humans in various settings, making our lives more comfortable and convenient.
Domestic service robots can vacuum floors, mow lawns, or even serve as companions by interacting with people.
In places like hospitals, service robots can transport medicines, deliver meals, and carry out simple medical tasks.

Module 5: Introduction to Robotics

Types of Robots

Humanoid Robots:

- Humanoid robots are designed to resemble the human form, with a head, torso, arms, and legs. They often have sensors and cameras to perceive their environment.
- These robots aim to mimic human movements and interact with people in a more human-like way.
- While still in development, humanoid robots hold potential in areas like assisting the elderly, disaster response, and even space exploration.

Pharmacy Robots:
- Pharmacy robots automate tasks in pharmacies, such as counting and dispensing medications.
- They help reduce the risk of medication errors and free up pharmacists' time to focus on patient consultations.
- Pharmacy robots can efficiently manage and organize medications, making sure patients receive the right dosage at the right time.

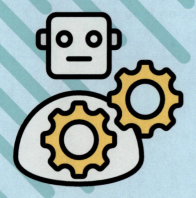

Module 5: Introduction to Robotics

How Robots Work

Robots may seem like magical machines, but in reality, they operate based on fascinating principles of science and technology. Understanding how robots work can be both exciting and enlightening. So, let's uncover the secrets of automation and learn how these incredible machines function:

Sensing the World:
Robots are equipped with various sensors that act as their eyes, ears, and touch.
These sensors help robots perceive their surroundings and collect information about the environment.
Examples of sensors include cameras for vision, microphones for hearing, and touch sensors to detect physical contact.

Processing Information:
The information collected by sensors is sent to the robot's "brain" called the controller or the computer.
The controller processes this information using complex algorithms and software programs.
It makes decisions based on the data received, determining the appropriate actions for the robot to take.

Making Decisions and Planning:
Once the controller processes the information, it decides what the robot should do next.
The robot's programming guides it to perform specific tasks based on the data and instructions received.
For example, if a robot senses an obstacle in its path, it will analyze the data and decide to change direction to avoid a collision.

Module 5: Introduction to Robotics

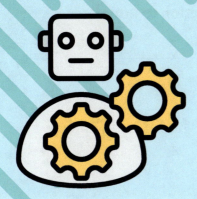

How Robots Work

Actuating Movements:
- Actuators are the robot's "muscles" responsible for moving its various parts and performing tasks.
- Motors and servos are common types of actuators used in robots.
- When the controller sends signals to the actuators, they respond by moving the robot's arms, legs, wheels, or other components.

Feedback Loop:
- To ensure accuracy and efficiency, robots often have a feedback loop system.
- This means the robot's sensors continuously send information back to the controller, allowing it to adjust its actions based on real-time data.
- For example, a robot vacuum cleaner might use its sensors to detect walls and obstacles, adjusting its path to navigate through the room smoothly.

Programming Robots:
- Robots are programmed using computer languages and coding.
- Robotics engineers and programmers write the code that tells the robot how to interpret sensor data and perform specific tasks.
- Programming robots involves creating logical sequences of instructions, such as "if-then" statements and loops.

Understanding how robots work allows us to appreciate the incredible blend of science, engineering, and computer programming that goes into creating these intelligent machines. As technology advances, robots will continue to become more sophisticated and capable, revolutionizing industries and enhancing our daily lives in remarkable ways.

Module 5: Introduction to Robotics

Robotics and AI:
The Power of Smart Machines

Robotics and Artificial Intelligence (AI) are two closely related fields that are transforming the world around us. While robotics deals with the design and construction of robots, AI focuses on creating intelligent machines capable of performing tasks that usually require human intelligence. Let's dive into the fascinating world of Robotics and AI and understand how they work together:

Robotics and AI Synergy:
Where Intelligence Meets Action

Robotics and Artificial Intelligence (AI) work together in perfect harmony, creating a powerful combination that brings robots to life with intelligence and adaptability. Imagine robots that can not only move and perform tasks but also learn, think, and make decisions like humans. That's the magic of Robotics and AI synergy!

AI, in simple terms, is about teaching machines to be smart and think for themselves. With AI, robots become more than just machines following instructions; they become smart machines that can perceive their environment, understand what they "see," and make decisions based on that understanding.

Through AI, robots can learn from their experiences and improve their performance over time. It's like they have their own brain, constantly growing and adapting. This is known as Machine Learning, where robots can recognize patterns, solve problems, and even predict outcomes without being explicitly programmed for each situation.

Module 5: Introduction to Robotics

Robotics and AI:
The Power of Smart Machines

Thanks to AI, some robots can operate **autonomously**, meaning they can function and make decisions without constant human guidance. Autonomous robots can navigate through complex environments, interact with objects, and complete tasks without continuous human intervention.

The synergy between Robotics and AI enables robots to interact with us in more human-like ways. They can understand our commands, respond to our questions, and even anticipate our needs. They become our helpful assistants, making our lives easier and more efficient.

The integration of Robotics and AI will continue to revolutionize industries and shape our future. As technology advances, we can expect to see more advanced robots capable of performing complex tasks, making our lives safer, easier, and more efficient.

Understanding the connection between Robotics and AI opens up a world of possibilities for creating intelligent machines that can transform industries, improve healthcare, and positively impact our lives. By embracing the power of smart machines and responsibly applying AI technologies, we can shape a brighter and more promising future for humanity.

In the future, we can expect even more exciting advancements in Robotics and AI. Imagine robots that can assist in complex medical procedures, explore distant planets, or help us during emergencies. The possibilities are endless, and this harmonious blend of Robotics and AI is shaping a future where smart machines work side by side with humans, transforming the way we live and interact with technology.

Module 5: Introduction to Robotics

Introduction to Robotics

QUIZ

1. What is robotics?

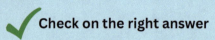 Check on the right answer

	a) The study of plants
	b) The study of robots and their applications
	c) The study of rocks and minerals

2. What part of a robot acts as its "eyes, ears, and touch"?

	a) Actuators
	b) Controllers
	c) Sensors

3. Which type of robot is commonly used in factories for assembling cars and electronics?

	a) Industrial robots
	b) Medical robots
	c) Service robots

Page: 101

Module 5: Introduction to Robotics

Introduction to Robotics

✓ Check on the right answer

4. What are the "muscles" of a robot responsible for moving its different parts?

a) Sensors
b) Actuators
c) Controllers

5. What is the name of the subset of AI that focuses on enabling machines to learn from data without explicit programming?

a) Machine Learning
b) Natural Language Processing
c) Deep Learning

6. Which type of robot can assist doctors in surgeries and perform tasks with high precision?

a) Industrial robots
b) Service robots
c) Medical robots

Module 5: Introduction to Robotics

Introduction to Robotics

✓ Check on the right answer

7. How do some robots understand human speech and respond to commands?

	a) Through sensors
	b) With the help of Machine Learning
	c) Natural Language Processing

8. What is the name of the subset of AI that focuses on enabling machines to learn from data without explicit programming?

	a) Machine Learning
	b) Natural Language Processing
	c) Deep Learning

9. Which type of robot can assist doctors in surgeries and perform tasks with high precision?

	a) Industrial robots
	b) Service robots
	c) Medical robots

Module 6:
Ethics and Artificial Intelligence

Module 6: Ethics and Artificial Intelligence

Ethics and Artificial Intelligence

As we delve deeper into the fascinating world of robotics and Artificial Intelligence (AI), we encounter a critical aspect that demands our attention: Ethics. Just like how humans have moral principles to guide their actions, robots and AI also require ethical considerations to ensure responsible and beneficial use.

Ethics is about making decisions that are fair, just, and considerate of the well-being of individuals and society as a whole. When we apply ethics to AI and robotics, we explore questions such as, "How do we ensure that robots make decisions that align with human values?" or "What are the implications of replacing human workers with robots in certain industries?"

AI-driven technologies are becoming increasingly prevalent, influencing various aspects of our lives. They help us in making decisions, offer personalized recommendations, and even automate tasks that would be challenging for humans alone. However, with such advanced capabilities, come ethical dilemmas that we need to address.

In this chapter, we will embark on a journey to explore the ethical considerations surrounding robotics and AI. We will discover how smart machines can impact privacy, jobs, and our interactions with technology. By understanding the importance of ethics in AI and robotics, we can ensure that we use these incredible technologies responsibly, shaping a future where smart machines and human society thrive together harmoniously. Let's navigate the moral path of smart machines together and explore the intriguing world of Ethics and AI.

Module 6: Ethics and Artificial Intelligence

Ethics and Artificial Intelligence

What is Ethics

Ethics is a fundamental concept that guides our behavior and helps us make good choices in our daily lives. It is like a compass that points us in the direction of what is right and wrong. Ethics teaches us how to be fair, honest, and considerate of others, ensuring that we act responsibly and with integrity.

At its core, ethics is about doing the right thing, even when nobody is watching. It involves making decisions based on principles and values that promote kindness, respect, and fairness. When faced with dilemmas, ethical thinking helps us weigh the consequences of our actions on ourselves and others, enabling us to choose the best course of action.

In our interactions with friends, family, and the community, ethics plays a vital role. It guides us to treat others with kindness and empathy, understanding that our actions can have a significant impact on the people around us. Being ethical means standing up for what is right, even if it's not the most popular choice, and being truthful, even when it is difficult.

Ethics extends beyond our personal lives; it also influences our behavior in the broader society and the world. In the digital age, ethics plays a role in how we use technology and social media responsibly. Respecting the privacy of others, avoiding cyberbullying, and using technology for positive purposes are all examples of ethical behavior.

In professional settings, ethics is vital in maintaining trust and integrity. Honesty, fairness, and respect for colleagues and customers build a strong foundation for ethical business practices.

Module 6: Ethics and Artificial Intelligence

Ethics and Artificial Intelligence

Fairness and Bias: Treating Everyone Equally in the Age of AI

Fairness is an essential aspect of ethics, and it becomes even more critical when we discuss Artificial Intelligence (AI) and smart machines. Fairness means treating everyone equally and without prejudice, regardless of their background, race, gender, or any other characteristic. In the context of AI, fairness ensures that AI systems and algorithms do not discriminate against any particular group or individual.

When developing AI models and algorithms, it is essential to use unbiased data and avoid perpetuating existing social biases. Sometimes, the data used to train AI systems may inadvertently contain biases that exist in society. For example, if an AI system is trained on historical data that reflects biased hiring practices, it may end up making biased decisions when used for recruitment.

Addressing fairness and bias in AI requires a careful and conscientious approach. AI developers and researchers must examine the data used for training, identify potential biases, and work to eliminate them. This process involves evaluating how different groups may be affected by AI decisions and ensuring that the outcomes are equitable for all.

One way to promote fairness in AI is by using diverse datasets that represent a wide range of perspectives and experiences. By including a variety of voices in the data, AI systems can better understand and cater to the needs of different communities.

Module 6: Ethics and Artificial Intelligence

Ethics and Artificial Intelligence

Fairness and Bias: Treating Everyone Equally in the Age of AI

Fairness is an essential aspect of ethics, and it becomes even more critical when we discuss Artificial Intelligence (AI) and smart machines. Fairness means treating everyone equally and without prejudice, regardless of their background, race, gender, or any other characteristic. In the context of AI, fairness ensures that AI systems and algorithms do not discriminate against any particular group or individual.

Additionally, transparency in AI decision-making is crucial. Users should have access to information about how AI systems arrive at their conclusions. This transparency enables individuals to understand the factors influencing AI decisions and allows for accountability in case biases are detected.

AI empowers new students learning AI to become responsible users and developers of technology. By learning to identify biases and advocate for fairness, they can contribute to building AI systems that uphold ethical principles.

Furthermore, promoting diversity in the fields of AI and technology is vital. Encouraging individuals from different backgrounds and perspectives to pursue careers in AI can lead to more inclusive and fair AI technologies.

In conclusion, fairness and bias are critical considerations in the development and deployment of AI. By actively working towards unbiased AI systems and being conscious of potential biases, we can create a more equitable and just society. Encouraging discussions on fairness in AI at a young age empowers the next generation to shape a future where smart machines promote fairness, equality, and inclusivity for all.

Module 6: Ethics and Artificial Intelligence

Ethics and Artificial Intelligence

Privacy Concerns: Safeguarding Personal Information in the Age of AI

Privacy is a fundamental right that ensures individuals have control over their personal information and how it is used. In the context of AI and technology, privacy concerns have become increasingly important as the amount of data collected and processed continues to grow. It is essential to address these concerns to protect individuals' rights and maintain trust in the use of AI systems.

With the advancement of AI, various applications, such as social media platforms, smart devices, and online services, gather vast amounts of data from users. This data includes personal information like names, addresses, preferences, and even behavioral patterns. While this data can be valuable for improving AI services, it also raises concerns about how it is being handled and who has access to it.

One significant concern is data breaches and cyberattacks. AI systems are powered by data, and any unauthorized access to this data can lead to severe privacy violations. Ensuring robust security measures, such as encryption and access controls, is crucial to protect personal information from falling into the wrong hands.

Moreover, the potential for data misuse and unauthorized sharing poses privacy risks. Organizations using AI should be transparent about how they collect and use personal data. Users should have the option to control what data is collected and to give explicit consent for its use.

Module 6: Ethics and Artificial Intelligence

Ethics and Artificial Intelligence

Privacy Concerns: Safeguarding Personal Information in the Age of AI

Privacy is a fundamental right that ensures individuals have control over their personal information and how it is used. In the context of AI and technology, privacy concerns have become increasingly important as the amount of data collected and processed continues to grow. It is essential to address these concerns to protect individuals' rights and maintain trust in the use of AI systems.

With the advancement of AI, various applications, such as social media platforms, smart devices, and online services, gather vast amounts of data from users. This data includes personal information like names, addresses, preferences, and even behavioral patterns. While this data can be valuable for improving AI services, it also raises concerns about how it is being handled and who has access to it.

One significant concern is data breaches and cyberattacks. AI systems are powered by data, and any unauthorized access to this data can lead to severe privacy violations. Ensuring robust security measures, such as encryption and access controls, is crucial to protect personal information from falling into the wrong hands.

Moreover, the potential for data misuse and unauthorized sharing poses privacy risks. Organizations using AI should be transparent about how they collect and use personal data. Users should have the option to control what data is collected and to give explicit consent for its use.

Module 6: Ethics and Artificial Intelligence

Ethics and Artificial Intelligence

Privacy Concerns: Safeguarding Personal Information in the Age of AI

Another privacy concern arises from the use of AI in surveillance and monitoring. While AI-powered surveillance systems can enhance security, they also raise questions about individual privacy and the potential for mass surveillance. Striking the right balance between public safety and personal privacy is essential to avoid infringing on individual rights.

Students should understand the importance of safeguarding their personal information and making informed decisions about sharing data online. By fostering a privacy-conscious mindset, young individuals can protect themselves and become responsible digital citizens.

In conclusion, privacy concerns in AI highlight the need to protect personal information while enjoying the benefits of AI technologies. By being aware of privacy risks and advocating for data protection, we can create a future where AI and privacy coexist harmoniously. Empowering the younger generation with knowledge about privacy concerns equips them to navigate the digital world safely and responsibly.

Module 6: Ethics and Artificial Intelligence

Ethics and Artificial Intelligence

Ethical Guidelines and Frameworks:

As Artificial Intelligence (AI) becomes more integrated into our lives, the need for ethical guidelines and frameworks to govern its use becomes increasingly apparent. Ethical guidelines are a set of principles and rules that guide individuals, organizations, and developers in creating and using AI in a responsible and fair manner. Here are some guidelines which are essential in shaping a future where smart machines and technology contribute positively to society.

Transparency and Explainability: Ethical guidelines emphasize the importance of transparency in AI systems. AI developers should ensure that users understand how AI technologies work and the factors that influence their decisions. Explaining the reasoning behind AI decisions can help build trust and accountability.

Avoiding Bias: Addressing bias in AI is crucial. Ethical frameworks encourage developers to use diverse and unbiased datasets during AI training to prevent discrimination and ensure fairness in outcomes. Students should understand the impact of biased data on AI systems and advocate for unbiased approaches.

Privacy and Data Protection: Ethical guidelines stress the significance of protecting user privacy and personal data. Developers should implement strong security measures to safeguard data from unauthorized access or breaches. Students should be aware of the data they share online and consider the importance of privacy in the digital age.

Module 6: Ethics and Artificial Intelligence

Ethics and Artificial Intelligence

Ethical Guidelines and Frameworks:

Human-Centered Design: Ethical frameworks emphasize designing AI systems that prioritize human well-being. AI should complement human abilities and enhance society rather than replace or harm individuals. Students can learn to assess AI technologies based on their positive impact on human lives.

Accountability and Responsibility: Ethical guidelines promote accountability for AI decisions and actions. Developers should take responsibility for the consequences of AI technologies and be proactive in addressing any potential harm. Students can advocate for responsible AI use and hold companies accountable for their actions.

Beneficial AI: The principle of beneficial AI centers on ensuring that AI technologies contribute positively to society. Ethical frameworks encourage the use of AI for purposes that benefit humanity, such as improving healthcare, education, and the environment. Students can think critically about the potential uses of AI and its impact on society.

Collaboration and Openness: Ethical guidelines highlight the importance of collaboration and sharing knowledge to promote responsible AI development. Open-source frameworks and cooperation between organizations can lead to more robust and trustworthy AI technologies. Students can engage in collaborative learning and share insights on ethical AI practices.

Continuous Learning and Adaptation: Ethical frameworks recognize that AI technologies evolve, and ethical considerations must adapt accordingly. Continuous learning and staying informed about the latest developments in AI ethics are essential for responsible AI use. Students can cultivate a mindset of lifelong learning and ethical awareness.

Module 6: Ethics and Artificial Intelligence

Ethics and Artificial Intelligence

QUIZ

✓ Check on the right answer

1. What are ethical guidelines and frameworks in AI intended to do?

	a) Encourage biased decision-making
	b) Promote fairness and responsible use of AI
	c) Limit the development of AI technologies

2. Why is addressing bias in AI important?

	a) To make AI systems more expensive
	b) To ensure fairness and prevent discrimination
	c) To make AI systems work faster

3. What does transparency in AI mean?

	a) Making AI systems complex and hard to understand
	b) Explaining AI decisions and how they are made
	c) Hiding AI algorithms from users

Module 6: Ethics and Artificial Intelligence

Ethics and Artificial Intelligence

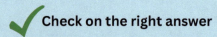 Check on the right answer

4. Why is protecting user privacy important in AI applications?

	a) To make AI systems more powerful
	b) To gain unauthorized access to user data
	c) To safeguard personal information and build trust

5. What does human-centered AI design prioritize?

	a) Replacing human jobs with AI robots
	b) Enhancing human abilities and well-being
	c) Ignoring human needs and preferences

6. What kind of purposes should AI be used for, according to ethical guidelines?

	a) Anything that generates the most profit
	b) Purposes that benefit humanity and society
	c) Solely for entertainment purposes

Module 6: Ethics and Artificial Intelligence

Ethics and Artificial Intelligence

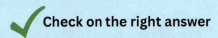

Check on the right answer

7. What does being responsible in AI use entail?

	a) Ignoring the consequences of AI decisions
	b) Advocating for biased AI algorithms
	c) Taking accountability for AI actions and their impact

8. Why is collaboration important in the context of AI ethics?

	a) To limit progress in AI technologies
	b) To share knowledge and promote responsible AI development
	c) To compete and withhold information from others

9. Why is continuous learning essential in AI ethics?

	a) To memorize AI algorithms
	b) To adapt ethical considerations to evolving AI technologies
	c) To become an AI expert

Glossaries

AI (Artificial Intelligence)

1. **Artificial Intelligence (AI):** The simulation of human intelligence in machines that can learn, reason, and perform tasks autonomously.
2. **Machine Learning:** A subset of AI that enables machines to learn from data and improve their performance without being explicitly programmed.
3. **Deep Learning:** A specialized form of machine learning that uses artificial neural networks to process and learn from vast amounts of data.
4. **Neural Networks:** Computational models inspired by the structure of the human brain, used in deep learning to process and analyze data.
5. **Reinforcement Learning:** A type of machine learning where an agent learns by interacting with an environment and receiving feedback in the form of rewards or penalties.

Natural Language Processing (NLP)

1. **Natural Language Processing (NLP):** The branch of AI that focuses on enabling computers to understand, interpret, and generate human language.
2. **Tokenization:** The process of breaking down text into smaller units, such as words or phrases, for analysis in NLP.
3. **Part-of-Speech Tagging:** Assigning grammatical categories (e.g., noun, verb, adjective) to words in a sentence using NLP techniques.
4. **Named Entity Recognition (NER):** Identifying and classifying named entities (e.g., names of people, organizations) in text using NLP.
5. Sentiment Analysis: Determining the sentiment or emotion expressed in text, whether positive, negative, or neutral, using NLP algorithms.

Glossaries

Machine Learning Glossary:

1. **Supervised Learning:** A type of machine learning where the algorithm is trained on labeled data, with input-output pairs provided for training.
2. **Unsupervised Learning:** A type of machine learning where the algorithm learns patterns and structures in unlabeled data without explicit guidance.
3. **Overfitting:** A situation in machine learning where a model performs well on training data but poorly on new, unseen data due to excessive complexity.
4. **Underfitting:** A situation in machine learning where a model is too simple to capture the underlying patterns in the data, resulting in poor performance.
5. **Feature Engineering:** The process of selecting, transforming, and creating relevant features from raw data to improve machine learning models.

Computer Vision Glossary:

1. **Computer Vision:** The field of AI that enables machines to interpret and understand visual information from images or videos.
2. **Image Classification:** Categorizing images into predefined classes using computer vision algorithms.
3. **Object Detection:** Identifying and locating objects within an image or video stream using computer vision techniques.
4. **Image Segmentation:** Dividing an image into meaningful segments or regions to facilitate further analysis and understanding.
5. **Convolutional Neural Network (CNN):** A type of deep learning model widely used in computer vision tasks, particularly for image analysis.

Ethics in AI Glossary:

1. **Bias:** Systematic errors or prejudices in AI algorithms that lead to unfair or discriminatory outcomes.
2. **Transparency:** The principle of making AI decision-making processes and algorithms understandable and explainable to users.
3. **Privacy Concerns:** Ethical considerations regarding the protection and responsible use of personal data in AI applications.
4. **Accountability:** Taking responsibility for the actions and consequences of AI systems and ensuring they align with ethical guidelines.
5. **Fairness:** Treating all individuals and groups impartially and without discrimination in AI decisions and outcomes.

End of the Book

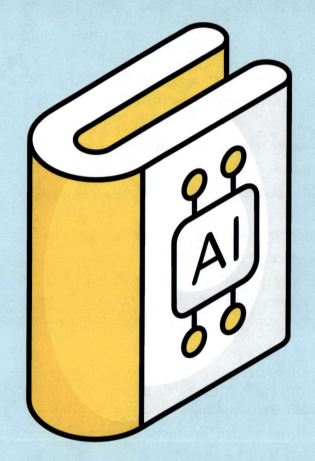

Thanks for Reading

Manufactured by Amazon.ca
Bolton, ON

35587479R00068